ART AT AUCTION 1981–82

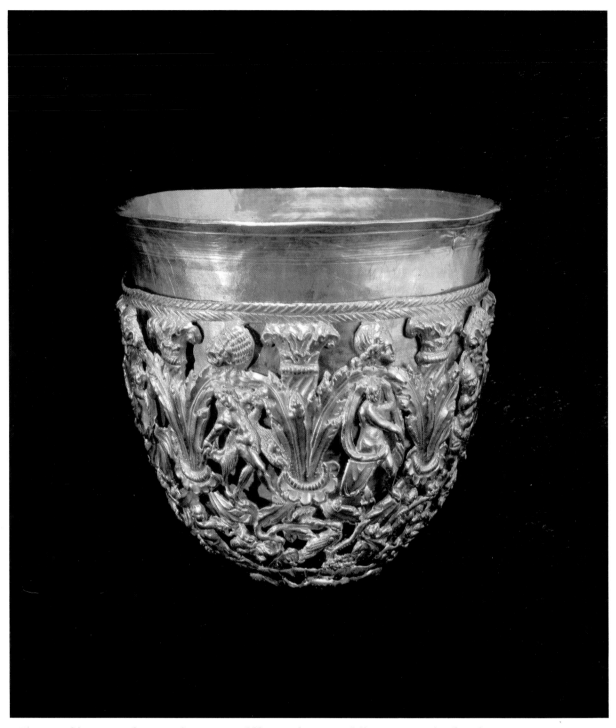

A Roman gold open-work cup with an inner gold lining, dioecesis of Illyricum or Italia, fourth century AD, diameter of cup 4¾in (12cm)
New York $198,000 (£110,615). 9.XII.81

The cup depicts members of the retinue of Dionysus and perhaps served a ceremonial function at an October festival of the god celebrating the vintage

ART AT AUCTION
The year at Sotheby's 1981-82

Two hundred and forty-eighth season

SOTHEBY PUBLICATIONS

First published for Sotheby Publications by
Philip Wilson Publishers Ltd,
Russell Chambers, Covent Garden, London WC2E 8AA
and
Sotheby Publications,
Biblio Distribution Centre,
81 Adams Drive, Totowa, New Jersey 07512

ISBN 0 85667 165 7
ISSN 0084-6783

Editor: Tim Ayers
Consultant editor: Joan A. Speers
Assistant (London): Jocelyn Stanton
Assistant (New York): Elizabeth White

Printed in England by Jolly & Barber Ltd, Rugby
and bound by R. J. Acford, Chichester

Note
Prices given throughout this book include the buyer's
premium, as applicable in the saleroom concerned. These
prices are shown in the currency in which they were realized.
The sterling and dollar equivalent figures for prices this
season, shown in brackets, are for guidance only and are
based on the rounded rates of exchange on 1 June 1982.
These rates for each pound sterling are as follows: United
States dollars, 1.79; Hong Kong dollars, 10.30; French francs,
10.96; Swiss francs, 3.58; Dutch guilders, 4.65; Italian lire,
2,328; South African rand, 1.93

The designations 'London' and 'New York' include all the
salerooms in these two places: Bond Street, Belgravia and
Bloomfield Place in London; Madison Avenue, York Avenue
and 84th Street in New York

Contents

DANIEL MACLISE, RA
Self portrait
Watercolour heightened with white over pencil with scratching out, signed and inscribed *by himself*, 7¼in by 5½in (18.4cm by 14cm)
London £12,100 ($21,659). 8.VII.82
From the collection of Mrs E. C. L. Copner

A Ming blue and white jar (*guan*), four character mark and period of Xuande, height 20⅜in (51.7cm)
London £792,000 ($1,417,680). 15.XII.81

The first Astor at Hever Castle

Clive Aslet

When William Waldorf Astor bought Hever Castle (Fig 1) in 1903, he restored the drawbridge and had it pulled up at night. A preoccupation with privacy undoubtedly provided one motive for buying the place. He already owned Cliveden in Buckinghamshire, which he had acquired from the Duke of Westminster. There he built a ten-foot wall around the park and stopped the public boating on the lake, giving rise to the joke that his middle name was really 'Walled-off'. In London, he did not sleep in his house in Carlton House Terrace, even after his own parties, but made his way to the Astor Estate Office on the Embankment – a jewel box of a building in the French Gothic style, designed by the architect of Truro Cathedral, John Loughborough Pearson. 'Here at least I am safe', he mysteriously told Lady Warwick when he gave her a tour of the building.

Lady Warwick knew Astor well and, remembering him in her book *Afterthoughts*, was forcibly struck by symptoms of what, today, would be taken as something verging on paranoia. In one of the upstairs rooms at the Estate Office he pointed to a lever by the side of his chair. 'If I were to press that,' he said, 'every door in the house would close and you could not possibly get out without my permission.' Then he smiled as he added: 'You have nothing to be uneasy about, as you know, but I must take precautions.' At Hever, smart young detectives who might have been mistaken for house guests patrolled the grounds every night.

It is not entirely surprising that Astor shrank from publicity. Although he bought both *The Pall Mall Gazette* and *The Observer*, he was dogged by a bad press. He was even criticized for having entertained too lavishly during the time he was American minister at Rome, during the early 1880s, because, as he recalled in his memoir *Silhouettes*, it put the post 'beyond the occupation of anyone without private means'. For a former diplomat he was strangely tactless, incensing his fellow countrymen by his widely reported comment on leaving the United States in 1893: 'America is not a fit place for a gentleman to live.'

But that was only one side of the man. Astor was also game enough to take his revenge on the American press by having the Astor Estate Office announce his death prematurely, with the result that he could read glowing tributes on every front page in New York. Restoring Hever gave him the excuse for another tease, by allowing no public admittance while work was in progress. He knew perfectly well, as he himself wrote in an unsigned article called 'Hever Restored' in *The Pall Mall Magazine* of 1907, that 'since the estate passed into the hands of the present owner many fantastic

Fig 1
Hever Castle, Kent. Much of the moated castle was built in the late fourteenth century, but it was William Waldorf Astor who undertook the restorations and improvements which have left the interior, out-buildings and extensive grounds in their present form

stories have found their way into print'. It evidently amused him to think that no one beyond those directly engaged on the project knew what lay behind the forest of scaffolding poles that had sprung up around the castle. Photographs were forbidden and each workman had to show a special pass to get on and off the site. Eight detectives worked in shifts around the clock to repel intrusive reporters.

Rumour on this occasion was hardly outdone by fact. A small army was engaged on the work. In December 1904, even before excavating the lake, which alone employed 800 navvies for two years, no less than 748 workmen were in Astor's employ at the castle. It was one man's job simply to carry forty-five gallons of beer to Hever every day for them to drink. Work was on the most lavish Edwardian scale – and Hever was only a second home.

The story of the Astor fortune is an American legend. The family originated in the village of Waldorf, near Heidelberg. At about the time of the American War of Independence, John Jacob Astor, the fifth son of a butcher, left to become a musical instrument maker in London, and then set off for the New World taking with him five pounds in cash and some instruments with which to open a business. An extra-ordinary meeting diverted his course. The brig that he crossed on, the *North Carolina*, became ice-bound in Chesapeake Bay with a number of other ships. Passengers walked from one to another over the ice, and it was in this way that Astor met a young fellow German who traded in furs. He saw that the business was lucrative and soon entered the fur trade himself. He was able to make a profit in London of 1,000 percent on skins that the Iroquois Indians on the Canadian border were happy to part with in exchange for cooking pans and pocket knives.

A portrait of John Jacob Astor hung in the library at Hever. It was copied from one painted in 1794, when he was reputed to be worth over $50,000. Profits were even greater after 1800, when the Napoleonic Wars forced him to look for new markets and he began trading with China. The surplus was invested in land. It was an obvious enough decision perhaps – but what land! Astor bought farms on the edge of the expanding port of New York. He began with a half share in the seventy-acre Eden estate, which cost him $70,000: it ran from what is now Broadway to the Hudson River just north of 42nd Street. Newspapers at the time of his death estimated that he was the richest man in America by far.

William Waldorf, John Jacob's great-grandson, was not cast in the family mould. Although he remembered that his father had never taken a holiday beyond the week-end for seventeen years, he himself hated business. He once described his joyless childhood in a letter: 'I was myself brought up severely and kept upon a pitiful allowance [from coming of age until he was twenty-five he received the comparatively meagre figure of $1,800 a year] . . . The hellfire sermons of my childhood, the like of which no congregation out of Scotland would listen to today, frightened me silly and I knew those red hot things were being made ready for *me*.' Having been intro-duced to Greek philosophy by his German tutor at the age of eighteen, he rebelled against the Calvinist ethic, embarked on a life-long love affair with Italy and became a passionate romantic, writing terrible novels with titles such as *Sforza* and *Valentino* and dialogue full of Renaissance idioms like: 'By the keys of St Peter, you send me upon a thorny quest.'

Fig 2
The inner courtyard of the castle, as it appeared shortly after William Waldorf Astor's restoration
Reproduced courtesy of *Country Life*

Fig 3
The inner hall and its ornate wood-carving, including the screen of columns whose history Astor
described in *The Pall Mall Magazine*

One major fruit of his romanticism – and particularly of his romantic, novelistic
attitude towards history – was the restoration of Hever, childhood home of Anne
Boleyn. The piquant detail, the curious fact were themes for his imagination to play
upon. Many pieces in the collection were acquired for their associational value as
much as for their inherent beauty. Typical is the layette worked, according to tradition, by the future Elizabeth I for the expected child of her half-sister Mary Tudor

and Philip II of Spain. Even the richly carved screen of columns in the inner hall of the castle had a story to tell (Fig 3). According to the article in *The Pall Mall Magazine*, the columns were made from a tree cut down in Caserta in 1747, which was later turned into a wine-press. 'Fire and tempest, the lightning's blast it escaped: wars and revolutions left it untouched.' Finally it was bought by the timber merchant who sold it to Astor. 'Nor, indeed, does its history end here, for a piece of an ancient rapier was found embedded in its heart, a romantic circumstance which our imaginations may interpret as they will.'

His masterstroke of romance, however, was the Tudor village, designed by J. L. Pearson's son, Frank. Providing guest rooms was a genuine problem. As Astor explained: 'It is impossible to add to a castle . . . yet if the rites of hospitality were to be exercised at Hever, some considerable extension was, of course, necessary.' The solution was to build a new wing on the other side of the moat, looking as though it was a cluster of houses on a medieval street. To keep up the fiction, different parts were given names like Cobham Corner, Medley Cottage and the Smuggler's Room. Masons and timber merchants in Kent still talk of how the Home Counties were scoured for old tiles, so that the 'village' should look genuinely old. Once again, Astor, writing in the guise of 'A Visitor', described the expected response: 'For a moment I could not believe that they had been built a few short months ago, they seemed so old and crooked, and possessed such individuality as though they had grown up one by one in various ages, as those old villages did which we sometimes see on our travels, sheltering themselves under the walls of the overlord.' This was Astor on one of his greatest flights of fancy. Some, it is true, also said that the arrangement reflected a desire to keep his guests at arm's length!

To some, the rich craftsmanship and exotic woods of the interior, with its carving by Nathaniel Hitch and William S. Frith, killed the very romance Astor so much enjoyed. Very different was Lindisfarne, another castle, off the Northumbrian coast, restored by Lutyens the year Hever was bought. There, remoteness and smoking fires and even a certain discomfort (Lytton Strachey shuddered at the stone passages and dawn fishing expeditions) were all part of the fun. But Astor, having 'no desire to call up from the past the phantoms of Plague, the Black Death, or the Sweating Sickness, and other deadly dwellers in the castle of the Middle Ages', turned Hever into an Edwardian country house, with all the provisions for personal cosseting that implies.

Astor's vision was certainly not as impractical as it at first appears. Until recently, Hever turned out to be particularly well suited to the late-twentieth-century needs of the family. The castle and gardens could be shown to the public, receiving some 144,000 visitors a year. The Tudor village, with its smaller, more comfortable rooms, provided a secluded home for family and guests. Few other Edwardian country houses have proved as adaptable.

During the past season, Sotheby Parke Bernet Realty Corporation and Savills of London were appointed international selling agents for the Hever Castle estate and art collection, which the trustees of the Lord Astor of Hever have decided to put up for sale.

Paintings and drawings

CRISTOFORO DA BOLOGNA
The Descent from the Cross
On panel, $22\frac{7}{8}$in by $14\frac{1}{8}$in
(58cm by 36cm)
London £115,500 ($206,745).
21.IV.82

GIOVANNI DI PAOLO
St John the Baptist disputing with the priests and Levites
On panel, 11¾in by 15¾in (30cm by 40cm)
Monte Carlo FF 1,026,750 (£93,682:$167,691). 13.VI.82
From the collection of Madame de Vienne; and now in the Musée du Petit Palais, Avignon

BARTOLOMEO PASSAROTTI
Portrait of a gentleman
45¼in by 36in (115cm by 91.5cm)
Florence L89,600,000 (£38,488:$68,894). 14.V.82

Traditionally this portrait is said to be of Marco Antonio Colonna (1535–88), who fought at the Battle of Lepanto in 1571

ALESSANDRO ALLORI
Portrait of a young man
On panel, signed and dated *M.D.L.XI*. twice, 52⅜in by 41in (133cm by 104cm)
London £82,500 ($147,675). 21.IV.82
From the collection of Bradford Walker; and now in the Ashmolean Museum, Oxford

JACOPO ROBUSTI called IL TINTORETTO
Portrait of a bearded man
25¾in by 19¾in (65.5cm by 50cm)
London £143,000 ($255,970). 23.VI.82

GIOVANNI FRANCESCO BARBIERI called IL GUERCINO
The penitent Magdalen
91in by 70½in (231cm by 179cm)
London £101,200 ($181,148). 9.XII.81

This picture was painted in 1649 for Cardinal Fabrizio Savelli, Legate of Bologna from 1648–51

ANTONIO CANALE called CANALETTO
Venice: a view from the Fondamenta Nuove
55⅞in by 59¼in (142cm by 150.5cm)
London £187,000 ($334,730). 23.VI.82
From the collection of the Rt Hon the Earl of Wharncliffe

Opposite
JACOB SAVERY THE ELDER
A kermesse
On panel, 10in by 14¾in (25.4cm by 37.5cm)
New York $137,500 (£76,816). 21.I.82
From the collection of the late Walter Stein

FRANCESCO GUARDI
A caprice with a ruined arch and a tempietto; A landscape caprice with Roman ruins
A pair, each 18½in by 13⅝in (47cm by 34.5cm)
London £121,000 ($216,590). 23.VI.82

BARENT AVERCAMP
A skating scene
On panel, 12in by 21$\frac{5}{8}$in (30.5cm by 55cm)
London £61,600($110,264). 21.IV.82

Opposite, above
QUIRIN GERRITSZ. VAN BREKELENKAM
A woman and children making lace
On panel, signed and dated *1654*, 24$\frac{1}{2}$in by 34in (62.2cm by 86.4cm)
New York $85,250(£47,626). 21.I.82

Opposite, below
JAN STEEN
Peasants making merry
Signed, 24$\frac{1}{2}$in by 30$\frac{1}{4}$in (62.2cm by 76.8cm)
New York $67,500(£37,710). 17.VI.82
From the collection of the Metropolitan Museum of Art, New York

HANS VON AACHEN
An assembly of the gods
On metal, 14⅛in by 18¼in (36cm by 46.5cm)
London £75,900 ($135,861). 21.IV.82
From the collection of Mr and Mrs B. von Reis

FRANCOIS BOUCHER
Venus sleeping
Signed, 46⅛in by 74¾in (117cm by 190cm)
Monte Carlo FF888,000(£81,022:$145,029). 26.X.81
From the collection of the late Lady Deterding

LOUIS–LEOPOLD BOILLY
A girl ironing
Signed, 15¾in by 12½in (40cm by 31.7cm)
London £51,700 ($92,543). 9.XII.81

JEAN-ETIENNE LIOTARD
The painter's son at breakfast
Circa 1770, 25in by 27¾in (63.5cm by 70.5cm)
London £297,000 ($531,630). 9.XII.81
From the collection of Monsieur Thierry Naville

This painting was exhibited at the Royal Academy in 1774

GIOVANNI BENEDETTO CASTIGLIONE
called IL GRECHETTO
St Mark
Brush drawing in brown, red-brown, blue, pink
and white paint, *circa* 1655–60, 14$\frac{3}{8}$in by 9$\frac{3}{4}$in
(36.4cm by 24.7cm)
London £19,250($34,458). 25.III.82
Now in the Los Angeles County Museum

WILLEM VAN DE VELDE THE ELDER
Dutch ships under sail with others at anchor
Grey wash over black chalk, 9$\frac{1}{2}$in by 17$\frac{1}{8}$in
(24cm by 43.4cm)
Amsterdam DFl 33,640(£7,234:$12,949).
19.IV.82

This is one of over fifty drawings by the elder
and younger Van de Velde discovered in an
English private collection, containing studies of
specific ships as well as views of naval actions
off England and Holland. The group was sold in
Amsterdam on 19 April 1982

DIRK HELMBRECKER
Study of a boy seated at a table
Red chalk, $12\frac{1}{8}$in by 8in (30.7cm by 20.2cm)
Amsterdam DFl 85,840 (£18,460:$33,043).
19.IV.82

JAN LIEVENS
An artist sketching in a wood
Pen and brown ink, $9\frac{1}{2}$in by $14\frac{1}{4}$in (24cm by 36.2cm)
Amsterdam DFl 40,600 (£8,731:$15,628).
19.IV.82

GIULIO CESARE PROCACCINI
The Entombment
Black chalk heightened with white on blue paper, $9\frac{1}{4}$in by $5\frac{7}{8}$in
(23.6cm by 14.9cm)
London £13,750($24,613). 25.III.82
Now in the Metropolitan Museum of Art, New York

This drawing is a study for Giulio Cesare's earliest known oil
painting, delivered in 1604, in S Maria presso S Celso, Milan

Below
GIOVANNI PAOLO PANINI
Two views of figures among classical ruins
A pair, pen and black ink and watercolour heightened with white,
each signed, each approximately 14in by $9\frac{3}{8}$in (35.7cm by 23.9cm)
London £18,700($33,473). 25.III.82
Now in the Pierpont Morgan Library, New York

HUBERT ROBERT
Garden of the Villa Aldobrandini at Frascati
Red and black chalk, 14in by 18½in (35.7cm by 47cm)
New York $38,500 (£21,508). 30.IV.82
From the collection of the late Christian Humann

JOHANN HEINRICH FUSELI, RA
The young Milton being taught by his mother
Circa 1796–99, 56in by 47in (142cm by 119cm)
Zurich SFr 107,800 (£30,112:$53,900). 30.XI.81

Opposite
SIR WILLIAM BEECHEY, RA
Portrait of Mrs Raymond Symons and her family
101in by 70in (256.6cm by 177.7cm)
London £45,100 ($80,729). 9.XII.81

This painting was exhibited at the Royal Academy in 1803

Hermia and Helena
by Washington Allston

William H. Gerdts

Washington Allston (1779–1843) is recognized today as one of the most significant and innovative American artists of the Romantic movement, the only one to achieve a truly international reputation. In his own lifetime, his works were discussed and admired in Germany, Italy and particularly in Great Britain. In his native land, contemporaries often wrote about him as the greatest American painter of the age. Allston's British fame was established during his second and longer stay in England, between the years 1811 and 1818, when he painted his most significant Grand Manner biblical dramas, some of his finest portraits and a number of attractive landscapes, as well as occasional genre pieces. It was also in this period that he developed the figural style which would culminate in his best-known and most admired later American works, the images referred to today as his 'dreamy women'.

A key picture in this figural development was his *Hermia and Helena* (Fig 1). The painting had been lost to public view until Sotheby's sale in December 1981, and it is probably the artist's most significant painting to reappear in recent years. *Hermia and Helena* was exhibited at the Royal Academy in 1818, but it may date from somewhat earlier. Allston's friendship and dealings with Harman van Schlyk Visger (1768–1833), who acquired the picture, seem to centre around 1813–14, the period of Allston's visits to Bristol, Visger's place of residence. The picture remained in the Visger family until the recent auction and family tradition suggests that Hermia and Helena are likenesses of two of Visger's many daughters, one of whom was named Helena; but such information is often unreliable.

Visger patronized not only Allston, but also Allston's pupil, Samuel F. B. Morse, who had accompanied Allston on the journey from New York to Liverpool in 1811. It was during the trip, on board the *Lydia*, that Allston and Morse met a Captain Visger. He provided an introduction to his cousin, Harman, and thus set the course for their Bristol patronage.

In Bristol, Allston was visiting John King, a noted surgeon, for medical treatment. King was also the most important local amateur of the arts and, besides the introduction to Visger, another amateur, Allston was no doubt keen to strengthen ties with his uncle Elias Vanderhorst, the American Consul there.

From his correspondence with Allston and Morse, Harman Visger seems to have been sensitive to critical opinion; in the case of *Hermia and Helena*, he must have

Fig 1
WASHINGTON ALLSTON, ARA
Hermia and Helena
Circa 1814–18, 29¾in by 25in (75.6cm by 63.5cm)
London £115,500 ($206,745). 9.XII.81
From the collection of Mrs M. E. Pearce

Fig 2
WASHINGTON ALLSTON, ARA
The valentine
1809–11, 25½in by 22in (64.8cm by 55.9cm)
From a private collection

found reassurance in the comments made on its appearance at the Royal Academy. The *Examiner*, almost always favourable to Allston, spoke well of the picture, the critic writing on 7 June 1818: 'There is a pleasant sedateness of feeling excited by Mr Allston's Hermia and Helena [exhibition number] 140. Its unassuming colour and cheerful light, its elegant dresses and more elegant females, elegant in mind as well as person – its scene of seclusion, the connected position, studious and kindly looks of the young friends as they hold the same book to read from, give us a charming picture of friendship.' Allston and Morse's colleague, the Anglo-American artist, Charles Robert Leslie, wrote to Allston on 3 March 1820, after the latter had returned to Boston, that, 'Mr Visger is much pleased with your "Hermia and Helena". It hangs in his drawing room, Portland Square, Bristol.'

The subject is taken from Act II, scene 2 of Shakespeare's *Midsummer Night's Dream*. It is one of half a dozen painting subjects which Allston borrowed from Shakespeare, and one of several taken from this play; his unfinished *Titania's court* of 1837, at Vassar College, is another. Yet, the *Examiner* critic was quite perceptive. In *Hermia and Helena*, Allston is more concerned with the evocation of friendship than with literal pictorialization. As Allston wrote to his sculptor friend, John Cogdell, on 25 July 1831, when recommending the subject: 'I painted this subject when in England, and not thinking it essential to adhere to the letter, instead of the sampler [the object of their attention in the play] I made them reading together from the same book. I endeavoured to give the spirit, which is all I would recommend to you.'

Hermia and Helena represents the confluence of a number of directions in Allston's art. One is the strain of literary illustration, which also includes works after Washing-

Fig 3
WASHINGTON ALLSTON, ARA
The sisters
Circa 1814–18, 49½in by 38¾in (125.7cm by 98.4cm)
Reproduced courtesy of the Fogg Art Museum,
Mrs Edward W. Moore gift, Cambridge,
Massachusetts

Fig 4
BENJAMIN WEST, PRA
Fidelia and Speranza
1776, 54¾in by 42⅝in (139.1cm by 108.3cm)
Reproduced courtesy of the Timken Art Gallery,
Putnam Foundation Collection, San Diego,
California

ton Irving and Walter Scott. Another is Allston's development of pure figure painting, as opposed to story-telling genre or portraiture, a concern that in America was original to him and which would have repercussions in the work of younger American painters. It begins with *The valentine*, painted in 1809–11 when Allston was in Boston between his two European sojourns (Fig 2). The work was derived from a painting he had done of his young wife, Ann Channing Allston, but in *The valentine* Allston has translated the subject into a generalized image of charm, tenderness and reverie. Since much of his female imagery at this period bears a general resemblance to his wife, *Hermia and Helena* itself may well owe something to his touching devotion to his spouse, who died in London early in 1815, although it is probably not meant to contain her specific image.

The paintings closest to *Hermia and Helena* in style are also products of Allston's later London years. One is *The sisters*, in which he produced another *schwesterschaft* or *freundschaft* image, with an idyllic, intertwined pair of young women, again one blonde, one brunette (Fig 3). The contrast between the two is greater than in *Hermia and Helena* and programmatically so, for the blonde 'sister' is taken directly from Titian's *Girl holding a jewel casket*, while Allston claimed the dark-haired young woman seen from the back as his own creation. In *The sisters*, Allston is acknowledging his dependence upon Titian in both spirit and technique, and the original Allston figure is presented as dependent upon her more lively sister, just as Allston was dependent on the great Venetian master. Allston may also imply here his artistic debt to his own master, Benjamin West, who had adapted the same Titian figure and composition in his *Bacchante* of 1797. Finally, in the paired female figures of both *Hermia and Helena* and *The sisters*, Allston could have been inspired by West's *Fidelia and Speranza* of 1776, a two-figure group derived from Spencer's *Faerie Queene* (Fig 4). Such duality of female figures is usually associated with the German Romantic school, and recalls above all Friedrich Overbeck's *Germania and Italia*, but that work, begun in 1811 and only completed in 1828, could not have influenced Allston.

It is interesting to note that Allston treated this theme several more times. His unfinished *Dido and Anna* has in previous literature been related to his Roman years, 1805–8, because of its classical subject matter, but it may well also be a London production. An unlocated and presumably unfinished picture about which Allston wrote to Leslie in February 1823, was *Minna and Brenda on the seashore*, derived from Walter Scott's novel *The Pirate* of 1822. The subject of two women, united by birth and by their love for two brothers, suggests the possibility of treatment similar to that in *Hermia and Helena* and *The sisters*.

Although a single-figure subject, the work by Allston closest to *Hermia and Helena* is surely *Contemplation*, acquired by the 3rd Earl of Egremont and still in the Petworth Collection (Fig 5). In both pictures, the figures appear in a secluded landscape setting. The figure in *Contemplation* is especially close to the dark-haired woman in *Hermia and Helena*, and the painting of the foot and sandal of each is identical. In both works, the figures, though small in actual size, are quite heroic in their prominence within the landscape setting, and in their generalized treatment they suggest a massiveness derived ultimately from Michelangelo and Raphael, who were much admired by Allston. Perhaps they reflect more immediately the enthusiasm generated by the Elgin marbles. Yet, in this group of figural paintings, all of which date from *circa* 1814–18, Allston appears to be turning away from the explicitly heroic to more contemplative and poetic imagery. This is a direction paralleled in his biblical dramas, from the high tensions of his *Dead man restored to life by touching the bones of the prophet Elisha* of 1811–14, to the graceful poetry of his *Jacob's dream* of 1817, also acquired by the Earl of Egremont. This new emphasis upon lyrical evocation, so well embodied in *Hermia and Helena*, was to dominate Allston's pictorial interpretations during his later American years.

Fig 5
WASHINGTON ALLSTON, ARA
Contemplation
Circa 1814–18, 26in by 27¾in (66cm by 70.5cm)
Reproduced courtesy of the Lord Egremont and
Leconfield

SIR PETER LELY
Portrait of Arthur, Lord Capel, later 1st Earl of Essex, and his wife Elizabeth
Circa 1653, 48¾in by 65½in (123.8cm by 166.4cm)
London £24,200 ($43,318). 18.XI.81
From the collection of Paul Mellon; and now in the National Portrait Gallery, London

JACQUES-LAURENT AGASSE
The Wellesley Arabian with his owner and groom
Signed, *circa* 1809, 33½in by 43¼in (85.1cm by 109.8cm)
London £85,800 ($153,582). 9.XII.81
From the collection of Brigadier K. F. W. Dunn, CBE, DL

This was one of two horses of Persian–Arabian stock imported from India in 1803 by Henry Wellesley

JOHN FREDERICK HERRING SR
A gentleman on a bay hunter
Signed and dated *1843*, 27½in by 34¾in (69.9cm by 88.3cm)
London £72,600($129,954). 9.XII.81

Opposite
JOHN FERNELEY SR
Squire Wormald with the Bedale Hunt
Signed, inscribed *Melton Mowbray* and dated *1828*, 54in by 120in (137.2cm by 304.8cm)
London £137,500($246,125). 17.III.82

JAMES SEYMOUR
A lady and gentleman on horseback with a huntsman
Signed and dated *1738*, 39in by 49in (99.1cm by 124.5cm)
London £35,200 ($63,008). 7.VII.82
From the collection of the Cranfield Charitable Trust

RICHARD PARKES BONINGTON
Henry IV's bedchamber at the château of La Roche-Guyon
On board, *circa* 1825, 9in by 14in (22.9cm by 35.5cm)
London £28,600 ($51,194). 9.XII.81

Bonington painted a number of works based on the life of Henry IV, perhaps most notably *Henry IV and the Spanish Ambassador of circa* 1827. This is his earliest treatment of Henry IV at La Roche-Guyon, where the king stayed after the Battle of Ivry, 14 March 1590

FRANCIS DANBY, ARA
Sunset at sea after a storm
35½in by 56½in (90.2cm by 143.5cm)
London £63,800 ($114,202). 17.III.82
Now in the Bristol City Art Gallery

This painting was exhibited at the Royal Academy in 1824, and bought by Sir Thomas Lawrence, PRA

JOSEPH MALLORD WILLIAM TURNER, RA
Off Ramsgate
Circa 1840, 12¼in by 19in (31.1cm by 48.2cm)
London £154,000 ($275,660). 17.III.82
From the collection of Rugby School

This painting formed part of a group of pictures owned by Mrs Booth, with whom Turner lodged in Margate and who later became his housekeeper in Chelsea

JOHN ROBERT COZENS
The Lake of Nemi
Watercolour over pencil, signed, inscribed and dated *Rome 1779* on the mount, $14\frac{1}{4}$in by 21in
(36.2cm by 53.3cm)
London £18,700 ($33,473). 8.VII.82

Cozens painted this view of the Lake of Nemi during his first visit to Italy, when he travelled in the
company of Richard Payne Knight

JOHANN HEINRICH FUSELI, RA
Mrs Fuseli as a courtesan, wearing an elaborate head-dress
Grey and white wash and pink bodycolour over pencil, *circa* 1790–1800, 15¼in by 11¼in
(38.7cm by 28.5cm)
London £25,300 ($45,287). 18.III.82

WILLIAM BLAKE
Christ nailed to the Cross (*The Third Hour*)
Watercolour, pen and black ink over traces of pencil, signed with monogram, 13in by 13⅝in
(33cm by 34.6cm)
London £28,600 ($51,194). 8.VII.82
From the collection of Professor Yura Kimiyoshi

This watercolour is one of the earliest from a series illustrating episodes from the Bible, which were
commissioned by Blake's principal patron, Thomas Butts, and painted between 1799 and 1809

JOSEPH MALLORD WILLIAM TURNER, RA
The Pass of Stelvio
Watercolour over traces of pencil, inscribed and numbered *Stelvodia Pass/Stelvio? No 2* on a label
attached to the backboard, *circa* 1842, $11\frac{1}{4}$in by 9in (28.5cm by 22.8cm)
London £35,200 ($63,008). 19.XI.81
From the collection of the Rt Hon the Earl of Oxford and Asquith, KCMG

JOSEPH MALLORD WILLIAM TURNER, RA
Caerlaverock Castle
Watercolour, *circa* 1831, 3¾in by 5⅝in (9.5cm by 14.2cm)
London £28,600($51,194). 18.III.82

AUGUSTUS CHARLES DE PUGIN
Brighton Pavilion: the principal entrance, west front
Watercolour over pencil, inscribed and numbered *Principal Entrance/No 2* on the reverse of the
mount, *circa* 1817–18, 9in by 13¼in (22.8cm by 33.6cm)
London £5,500($9,845). 10.VI.82

JACQUES-JOSEPH TISSOT
The fan
Signed, early 1870s, 14½in by 19in (36.8cm by 48.2cm)
London £46,200 ($82,698). 15.VI.82

JOHN ATKINSON GRIMSHAW
Summer
Signed and dated *1875*, and signed and inscribed *Knostrop Hall, Leeds* on the stretcher, 24½in by 29½in
(62.2cm by 75cm)
London £50,600 ($90,574). 10.XI.81

The lady is Grimshaw's wife, Frances Theodosia, standing at the window in the morning room of their
house, Knostrop Old Hall, in Yorkshire

ABRAHAM SOLOMON
First class – The meeting
Signed and dated 1854, 27in by 38in (68.6cm by 96.5cm)
New York $132,000 (£73,743). 29.X.81

This painting is the second version of the subject: the first had caused outrage by showing the young couple flirting before her sleeping guardian. It is a sequel to *Second class – The parting*, in which a young son leaves his bereaved and impoverished mother

FREDERIC, LORD LEIGHTON, PRA
Melpomene, Muse of Tragic and Lyric Poetry; Terpsichore, Muse of Dance; Thalia, Muse of Comedy
Triptych, *circa* 1886, 65½in by 98¾in (166.4cm by 250.8cm)
London £121,000 ($216,590). 15.VI.82

These three canvases were developed from Lord Leighton's *Mythological triptych illustrating music* and were commissioned by Henry Gurdon Marquant, second President of the Metropolitan Museum of Art, New York, for his music salon

WILLIAM HOLMAN HUNT, OM
Amaryllis (*The shepherdess*)
On panel, signed with monogram, 1884–86, 25in by 19½in (63.5cm by 49.5cm)
London £50,600 ($90,574). 10.XI.81

This was one of several pictures whose aim Hunt described in his autobiography to have been, 'to give varying types of womanhood with unaffected innocence of sentiment'

DANTE GABRIEL ROSSETTI
Alexa Wilding
Coloured chalk, signed with monogram and dated *1873*, 26in by 23½in (66cm by 59.7cm)
London £39,600 ($70,884). 10.XI.81

Alexa Wilding frequently sat for Rossetti in the late 1860s and the 1870s. She is recognizable in such works as *Regina cordium* (1866) and *The blessed damozel* (1875–78)

JOHN MELHUISH STRUDWICK
Passing days
On panel, *circa* 1878, 15in by 45in (38.1cm by 114.3cm)
London £44,000 ($78,760). 10.XI.81

WALTER CRANE
The Laidley Worm of Spindleton Heugh
Signed with monogram and dated 1881, 29¾in by 66¾in (75.6cm by 169.6cm)
London £60,500 ($108,295). 15.VI.82

This subject is taken from a Northumbrian legend, in which a princess is transformed into a serpent by a wicked stepmother and then restored to her true form with a kiss. This gave rise to the *Ballad of Bamborough Castle*, whose last verse runs:

> He sheathed his sword and bent his bow,
> And gave her kisses three;
> She stept into a hole a worm,
> And stepped out a ladye

SIR ALFRED MUNNINGS, PRA
The Newmarket start
On panel, signed, 23in by 27in (58.4cm by 68.6cm)
New York $253,000 (£141,341). 27.V.82

HENRY LA THANGUE, RA
Leaving home
Signed and dated '89, 69in by 57½in (175.2cm by 146.1cm)
London £19,800 ($35,442). 10.XI.81

PAUL NASH
The steps
Signed and dated *1920–23*, 19¾in by 23½in (50.2cm by 59.7cm)
London £18,700($33,473). 10.III.82

LAURENCE STEPHEN LOWRY, RA
Going to work
Signed and dated *1952*, 23½in by 29½in
(59.7cm by 74.9cm)
London £35,750 ($63,993). 10.III.82

Right
SIR WILLIAM ROTHENSTEIN
Eric Gill and the artist's wife
Circa 1914, 41in by 37in (104.1cm by 94cm)
London £9,900 ($17,721). 19.V.82

CASPAR DAVID FRIEDRICH
A mountain peak with drifting clouds
Circa 1835, $9\frac{1}{4}$in by $11\frac{1}{2}$in (23.5cm by 29.2cm)
London £187,000 ($334,730). 25.XI.81

This is one of eight recorded oil paintings acquired from the artist by Count Friedrich von Hahn, and it bears the stamp of his seal on the stretcher

NICOLAS-ANTOINE TAUNAY
The harvest
19in by 23½in (48.2cm by 59.7cm)
New York $39,600 (£22,123). 25.II.82

LANCELOT-THEODORE TURPIN DE CRISSE
The Temple of Minerva, Athens
Signed and dated *1805*, 43in by 62¾in (109.2cm by 159.4cm)
London £39,600 ($70,884). 25.XI.81

This painting was exhibited at the Paris Salon of 1806. It was probably commissioned by the diplomat and architect, Choiseul-Gauffier, who was Turpin de Crissé's first sponsor and the author of one of the earliest works on modern Greece, the *Voyage Pittoresque de la Grèce* (1782)

Opposite
PIERRE-NOLASQUE BERGERET
Marius meditating on the ruins of Carthage
Signed with monogram and dated *AN 1807*, 51in by 38in (129.5cm by 96.5cm)
Monte Carlo FF 233,100 (£21,268:$38,070). 13.VI.82

IVAN KONSTANTINOVICH AIVAZOVSKY
A lifeboat being driven towards rocks
Signed and dated *1881*, 40$\frac{5}{8}$in by 51$\frac{3}{4}$in (103.2cm by 131.5cm)
London £26,400 ($47,256). 3.III.82

This painting was formerly in the collection of Queen Olga of the Hellenes, Grand Duchess of Russia

Opposite
BAREND CORNELIS KOEKKOEK
Cattle and figures in a forest
Signed and dated *1834*, 66$\frac{1}{2}$in by 57$\frac{1}{8}$in (169cm by 145cm)
Amsterdam DFl 394,400 (£84,817:$151,822). 17.XI.81

JEAN-LEON GEROME
Portrait of Marie Gérôme, née Goupil
Signed, *circa* 1870, 21¼in by 14¼in (54cm by 36.2cm)
London £45,100 ($80,729). 15.VI.82

Marie Gérôme, the artist's wife, was the daughter of the famous Paris art dealer,
Paul Goupil

ERNEST-ANGE DUEZ
Paris – at the restaurant Le Doyen
Signed, *circa* 1878, 34¾in by 45in (88.3cm by 114.3cm)
London £45,100 ($80,729). 25.XI.81

ANGELO MORBELLI
Women knitting
Signed, inscribed *a Primo Levi* and dated *1890*, 12¼in by 17⅜in (31cm by 44cm)
Florence L 39,200,000 (£16,838:$30,140). 13.V.82

JOAQUIN SOROLLA Y BASTIDA
Al baño, Valencia
Signed and dated *1908*, 40½in by 28½in (102.9cm by 72.4cm)
New York $170,500(£95,251). 29.X.81

LUDWIG DEUTSCH
The water seller
On panel, signed and dated *1891*, 16½in by 12¼in (41.9cm by 31.1cm)
London £39,600 ($70,884). 16.VI.82

TELEMACO SIGNORINI
Via Santa Maria de Bardi, Florence
Signed, *circa* 1870, 35in by 26in (88.9cm by 66cm)
New York $165,000 (£92,179). 29.X.81

CHARLES-EMILE JACQUE
A shepherd guarding his flock by a pond
Signed, 23¼in by 44in (59cm by 111.8cm)
New York $52,800 (£29,497). 29.X.81
From the collection of Lüchow's Restaurant, New York

JEAN-FRANCOIS MILLET
The sower
Pastel and black chalk, signed, *circa* 1865, 14$\frac{1}{8}$in by 16$\frac{7}{8}$in (35.9cm by 42.9cm)
New York $330,000 (£184,358). 27.II.82
From the collection of the late Roy J. Carver

CAMILLE PISSARRO
Vegetable gardens at l'Hermitage, Pontoise
Signed and dated *1873*, 21¼in by 28¾in (54cm by 73cm)
London £401,500 ($718,685). 30.VI.82

CLAUDE MONET
Pleasure boats at Argenteuil
Signed and dated *1875*, 21¼in by 25¾in (54cm by 65.4cm)
New York $1,430,000(£798,883). 5.XI.81

PIERRE-AUGUSTE RENOIR
The cup of tea
Signed, 1906–7, 31⅞in by 25¾in (81cm by 65.4cm)
New York $797,500 (£445,531). 5.XI.81

The seated figures are probably Georges Rivière, Renoir's close friend and biographer, and one of his
daughters, who often visited the artist at this period. The standing woman is Gabrielle, Renoir's model

EDGAR DEGAS
Seated bather drying herself
Pastel, signed, 20¾in by 20⅞in (52.7cm by 53cm)
New York $698,500 (£390,223). 5.XI.81
From the collection of Peter Fuller

PAUL SIGNAC
Collioure: les balancelles
Signed, inscribed *Op. 167* and dated *87*, 18in by 23¼in (45.7cm by 59cm)
London £195,800 ($350,482). 2.XII.81

This is one of four views of the port of Collioure painted between September and October 1887, and is among Signac's earliest *pointilliste* works

PAUL CEZANNE
Still life with apples and a napkin
Circa 1879–82, 19⅞in by 24⅛in (50.5cm by 61.2cm)
New York $1,980,000(£1,106,145). 5.XI.81

JAMES ENSOR
Melancholy fishwives
Signed and dated *1892*, 39⅜in by 31¼in (100cm by 79.4cm)
New York $385,000 (£215,084). 5.XI.81
From the collection of the late Anne Burnett Tandy

HENRI DE TOULOUSE–LAUTREC
Model resting after her bath
On board, signed, 1896, 25⅜in by 19¼in (64.4cm by 49cm)
London £759,000 ($1,358,610). 31.III.82

ARISTIDE MAILLOL
Summer
Bronze, signed and numbered *No 5*, *circa* 1910–11, height 64in (162.5cm)
New York $308,000 (£172,067). 5.XI.81
From the collection of Sam Salz

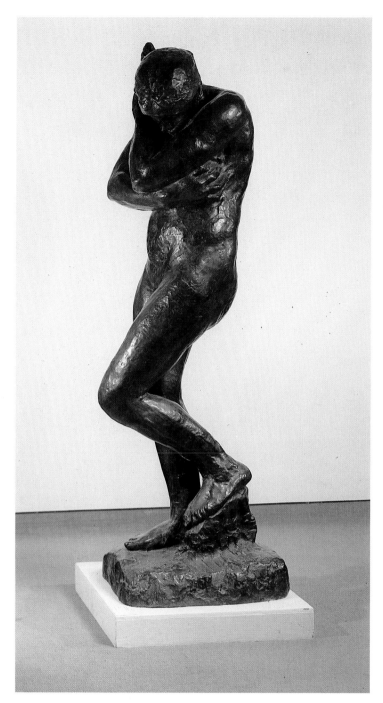

AUGUSTE RODIN
Eve
Bronze, signed and inscribed *Georges Rudier Fondeur Paris*,
height 68in (172.7cm)
New York $231,000 (£129,050). 22.V.82

The original model for this bronze was executed in 1881, shortly
after Rodin had completed his *Adam*

KEES VAN DONGEN
In front of the mirror
Signed, *circa* 1911, 39¼in by 31½in (99.7cm by 80cm)
London £308,000 ($551,320). 30.III.82

The avant-garde furniture in this painting is typical of the simple painted chairs and tables
manufactured by Paul Poiret's Atelier Martine, founded in 1911. He employed young girls and
encouraged them to express a fresh and naïve approach to decorative domestic design, giving
rise to products which are among the earliest forms of Art Deco

AMEDEO MODIGLIANI
Portrait of a young girl (Jeanne Huguette)
Signed, *circa* 1917–18, 36in by 23¾in (91.5cm by 60.3cm)
New York $847,000 (£473,184). 5.XI.81

EMIL NOLDE
Phantasie B
Watercolour, pen and indian ink, signed, *circa*
1931–35, 16in by 12in (40.6cm by 30.5cm)
London £50,600 ($90,574). 2.XII.81

Below
ERNST LUDWIG KIRCHNER
Olympia
Signed, *circa* 1914–15, 29in by 58½in (73.7cm
by 148.6cm)
London £99,000 ($177,210). 2.XII.81
From the Gustav Ferd. Jung Collection

Gustav Ferd. Jung (1878–1943) was a successful
German businessman and manufacturer. His
friendship with the artist Christian Rohlfs brought
him into contact with a number of the German
Expressionist painters and enabled him to form one
of the most important early collections of their
works. Many of the larger pictures and all his
correspondence with the artists were destroyed
during the Second World War, but the remainder
was sold in London on 2 December 1981

LYONEL FEININGER
The town hall at Swinemunde
Signed, 1912, 28in by 23¼in (71.1cm by 59cm)
New York $275,000 (£153,631). 5.XI.81

MARC CHAGALL
Bride and groom with the Eiffel Tower
Signed, 1928, 35in by 45⅝in (88.9cm by 115.9cm)
New York $660,000 (£368,715). 5.XI.81

LEON BAKST
The yellow sultana
Watercolour, gouache, charcoal and pencil heightened with gold, signed and dated *1916*,
18¾in by 27¼in (47.6cm by 69.2cm)
London £33,000 ($59,070). 4.III.82

GIORGIO DE CHIRICO
Metaphysical interior I
Signed, 1916, 12¾in by 10⅜in (32.3cm by 26.3cm)
New York $264,000 (£147,486). 5.XI.81
From the collection of the late Anne Burnett Tandy

PIET MONDRIAN
Composition in grey-blue
Signed, and signed and inscribed *Compositie 2* on the reverse, 31¼in by 25in (79.3cm by 63.5cm)
London £660,000 ($1,181,400). 30.III.82

Executed in Paris in late 1912 or early 1913, this painting was inspired by a group of sunflowers

SALVADOR DALI
Accommodations of desire
Oil and collage on board, signed and dated *29*, 8⅝in by 13¾in (21.9cm by 34.9cm)
New York $517,000(£288,827). 4.XI.81
From the collection of the late Julien Levy

According to the artist, this painting records 'visions inspired by a contemplation of pebbles on
the beach at Cadaquès' and in his memoirs he explains further: 'At this period I began to paint
Accommodations of desire, a painting in which desires were always represented by the terrorizing
images of lions' heads. "Soon you will know what I want of you", Gala [his wife] would say to me.
This could not be very different from my lions' heads, I thought, trying to accustom myself in advance
to the impending revelation by the most frightening representations'

ARSHILE GORKY
Study for 'Agony': two figures in an interior
Charcoal, pastel, pencil and gouache, *circa* 1947, 40in by 51¼in (101.6cm by 130.2cm)
New York $308,000 (£172,067). 4.XI.81
From the collection of the late Julien Levy

Julien Levy (1906–81) was introduced to the group around the Surrealists in Paris by Marcel
Duchamp, and in 1931 he opened a gallery in New York which played a key rôle in the introduction
of Surrealist works to the American public. His personal collection was sold in New York on
4 and 5 November 1981

HENRY MOORE, OM, CH
Reclining figure
Elm, 1945–46, length 75in (190.5cm)
New York $1,265,000 (£706,704). 20.V.82

The artist worked on this sculpture, for the Cranbrook Academy of Art, Michigan, concurrently with a reclining figure in Horton stone, for Dartington Hall, Devon. After 'two years of sculpture time I had lost through the war', he explains in his autobiography, 'I was able to satisfy both sides of my nature by working on the rather gentle Dartington figure at the same time as the Cranbrook Reclining Figure in elmwood, which for me had great drama, with its big beating heart like a great pumping station'

MARINO MARINI
Rider
Bronze, signed, 1951, height 47¼in (120cm)
London £143,000 ($255,970). 31.III.82

This is one of an edition of five

THOMAS MORAN
Big Springs in Yellowstone Park
Watercolour heightened with white, signed and dated *1872*, 9¼in by 19¼in (23.5cm by 48.9cm)
New York $187,000(£104,469). 23.IV.82

HENRY OSSAWA TANNER
The thankful poor
Signed, inscribed with the title and dated *1894*, 35½in by 44¼in (90.2cm by 112.4cm)
New York $275,000 (£153,631). 10.XII.81
From the collection of the Pennsylvania School for the Deaf, Philadelphia

On the reverse is a study for the painting *The sabot makers*

Opposite
ALFRED JACOB MILLER
Racing at Fort Laramie
Watercolour, signed, 7¾in by 12in (19.7cm by 30.5cm)
New York $101,750 (£56,844). 23.IV.82

The artist commented on Fort Laramie: 'This post was built by the American Fur Co situated about 800 miles West of St Louis ... Tribes of Indians encamp here 3 or 4 times a year, bringing with them peltries to be traded or exchanged'

William Merritt Chase – 'a typical American artist'

Ronald G. Pisano

The art of William Merritt Chase (1849–1916) has been described as dashing, spontaneous, masterly, bright, sensitive, vivacious, energetic and vital. Chase himself was considered by many contemporaries to be the quintessential American artist, embodying the true spirit and energy of America in everything he painted. Commenting on the predominant style of American painting at the time, one critic noted: 'The national style is a composite, blending indistinguishably the influence of old and new schools of painting . . . Mr Chase is a typical American artist.'[1] Duncan Phillips, the noted art collector, described Chase as 'the embodiment and epitome of that much underestimated phase of our life as a nation – our practical desire for beauty.'[2]

Chase was born in Indiana and, after a brief foray to New York to study at the National Academy of Design, he returned to the Midwest, where he supported himself by painting portraits and still lifes. In 1872, inspired by John Mulvaney, a fellow artist who had just returned from Europe, and supported by several prominent local businessmen, Chase decided to travel to Munich to complete his artistic training. His enthusiasm is apparent in his famous declaration: 'My God, I'd rather go to Europe than to heaven.'[3]

In a sense, Chase was reborn in Munich, where he revelled in the dashing, spontaneous and painterly approach of the faculty of the Royal Academy. Characterizing this vital group of painters, the American artist Kenyon Cox stated: 'All Munich men are enthusiastic lovers of art and of the great old masters.'[4] Certainly, Chase would refer to his training in Munich as the cornerstone of his artistic sensibility. In fact, Chase so embodied the spirit of the Munich school that he was asked to teach at the Royal Academy in 1878. He elected, instead, to return home, explaining later: 'I was young . . . American art was young; I had faith in it.'[5]

[1] Downes, W. H. 'William Merritt Chase, A typical American Artist', *The International Studio*, Vol XXXIX, no 154, December 1909, p xxix

[2] Phillips, D. 'William Merritt Chase', *The American Magazine of Art*, Vol VIII, no 2, December 1916, p 50

[3] Northrup, B. 'Great Artists's Struggle', *Indianapolis News*, 14 January 1899, p 9

[4] Cox, K. 'William M. Chase, Painter', *Harper's New Monthly Magazine*, Vol 78, March 1889, p 550

[5] 'Chase's Americanism', *Literary Digest*, Vol 53, 11 November 1916, p 1250

Fig 1
WILLIAM MERRITT CHASE
Shinnecock Hills, Peconic Bay
Signed, *circa* 1892–1902, 24in by 35¼in (61cm by 89.5cm)
New York $165,000(£92,179). 10.XII.81

The New York to which he returned in 1878 was in the throes of an artistic awakening, and Chase was determined to be involved. He joined the faculty of the newly established Art Students' League and, to everyone's surprise, managed to seize for himself the most prestigious studio space in the famous 10th Street studio. His career was off to a grand start. He was a colourful character and soon became a well-known figure about town, dressed in a cut-away coat, sporting a carnation in his buttonhole and wearing a scarf threaded through a jewelled ring. He also owned and showed off with great aplomb, several exotic pets, including a cockatoo and Russian wolfhounds. Somewhat short in stature, he compensated by wearing a top hat, which he adopted as the crown of his standard artistic garb. He was one of the most active artists of his day, full of energy and enthusiasm for any sort of artistic enterprise. He became a member of the important art organizations as well as more intimate clubs, including the Society of American Artists, the Society of Painters in Pastel, the

American Watercolor Society, the Art Club and the Tile Club. He was later elected to the National Academy of Design and the American Academy of Arts and Letters.

No doubt, his early emergence as the archetypal American artist of his day was in part due to the fact that he painted everyday life as it surrounded him, in and around New York. Only lately have his earlier paintings and pastels of the 1880s gained much acclaim, as witnessed by several works recently sold at auction, including *At the shore* (early 1880s) and *Gravesend Bay* (*circa* 1888) (see *Art at Auction* 1980–81, p154).

During the 1890s, Chase's work began to show the influence of French Impressionism; but unlike some other Americans who were easily overwhelmed by this foreign style, Chase was more cautious, adding a lighter palette to his already well-established painterly methods. Commenting on Chase's adaptation to French Impressionism, one critic noted: 'Few painters weathered the shock of Impressionism as he did.'[6] His tranquil renditions of the summer countryside and beaches are widely considered not only the high-point of his career, but the epitome of an American Impressionism (Figs 1, 3).

His championing of American art and the fact that he was one of the most influential American art teachers at the time also contributed to his image among contemporaries. The list of his prominent students reads like a *Who's Who* of twentieth-century American art, including such diverse artists as Georgia O'Keeffe, Joseph Stella, Marsden Hartley, Charles Demuth, Guy Pène du Bois, Rockwell Kent, Charles Hawthorne, Eugene Speicher and Kenneth Hayes Miller. In addition to teaching in New York, Chase gave classes in Philadelphia, Chicago and Hartford. However, his greatest influence as a teacher was as a result of the summer classes that he held at Shinnecock Hills, Long Island, between 1891 and 1902. It was here that he taught *plein-air* painting, encouraging so many of the next generation who were to be called American Impressionists.[7]

Chase was first and foremost an easel painter, but he was also proficient in watercolour, pastel and various forms of printmaking, including the monotype, which he elevated to the level of high art. Although his pastels are relatively few when compared to his many oil paintings, they are, without a doubt, of a consistently higher quality.

He was no less versatile in his choice of subject matter. He is credited with having made a significant contribution to the history of American art 'in his painting of the figure in relationship to its environment',[8] both in his landscape paintings and in his interior scenes. He was a successful portrait painter (Fig 2) with many commissions from the notables of the day. His characterization of James Abbott MacNeill Whistler (1885) is probably one of the best-known American portraits, apart from Whistler's own portrait of his mother. Chase also executed a series of self portraits that span his career and the various media in which he worked. Significantly, the Uffizi Gallery in Florence honoured Chase by including him among the very few American artists

[6] Butler, H. R. 'Chase – The Artist', *Scribner's Magazine*, Vol 61, February 1917, p 256
[7] He conducted another summer art class in 1914 at Carmel-by-the-Sea, California
[8] Roof, K. M. 'William Merritt Chase: An American Master', *Craftsman*, Vol 18, April 1910, p 38

Fig 2
WILLIAM MERRITT CHASE
A lady in brown
Signed, 20½in by 16¼in (52.1cm by 41.3cm)
New York $93,500. 4.XII.80

commissioned to paint their likenesses for the gallery's famous collection of self portraits. As a still-life painter, he was unsurpassed in America and was compared favourably to foreign artists. In a moving obituary, Duncan Phillips wrote: 'And yet when the history of the period is written by a critic yet unborn, it may be that he will write that this same Chase rivalled Chardin in painting fruits and vegetables, and Vollon in painting copper and brass and that he is unequalled by any other painter in the representation of the shiny, slippery fishiness of fish.'[9]

While Chase was obviously intent upon creating his own statement, and that statement was unabashedly American, he respected the European traditions of art, especially in terms of technique. 'I set myself to learn my trade – I am not afraid of the phrase' he said, 'and I made up my mind that if I was ever to do anything, it would be through making myself a master of the medium as the great men of the old time were.'[10]

It would therefore be wrong to conclude that Chase was in any way myopic in regarding the art of Europe or the divergent trends in art around the turn of the century. Chase was, in fact, a major figure on the international art scene; he travelled to Europe many times, visiting fellow artists, including Giovanni Boldini, John Singer Sargent, James Abbott MacNeill Whistler, John Lavery, Frank Brangwyn, Sir Lawrence Alma-Tadema and Joaquín Sorolla y Bastida. He exhibited regularly and won many awards and medals in international exhibitions, such as the Crystal Palace Exhibition in Munich, the Exposition Universelle in Paris, and the Exposición International de Belles Artes in Santiago, Chile. He also conducted summer classes in Europe, escorting his pupils to London, Madrid, Bruges, Venice and Florence. He even purchased a villa in Fiesole, outside Florence.

In 1902, as a tribute to Chase, his students commissioned John Singer Sargent to paint his portrait, which was then given to the Metropolitan Museum of Art. This was an apt choice by his students since Sargent and Chase, in addition to being friends, were considered kindred spirits. One critic, who noted this bond, stated: 'But to the Velasquez style, both Sargent and Chase have added a distinctly American something – the nervousness, crispness, intensity of American life. And that makes American art.'[11] It is this vitality, confidence and optimism that we find so appealing in Chase's work today.

[9] Phillips, p 49
[10] Chase, W. M. 'The Import of Art', *The Outlook*, Vol 95, 25 June 1910, p 442
[11] 'The Chase Exhibition', *The Outlook*, Vol 94, 29 January 1910, p 230

Fig 3
WILLIAM MERRITT CHASE
Sunny day at Shinnecock Bay
On panel, signed, 1892, $18\frac{1}{2}$in by $22\frac{3}{4}$in (47cm by 57.8cm)
New York $286,000. 4.XII.80

JOHN SINGER SARGENT
Portrait of Dorothy
Signed and dated *1900*, 24in by 19¾in (61cm by 50.2cm)
New York $286,000 (£159,777). 10.XII.81

GEORGE LUKS
Lily Williams
Signed, *circa* 1909, 44¾in by 39½in (113.7cm by 100.3cm)
New York $258,500 (£144,413). 10.XII.81
From the collection of the late Roy J. Carver

CHARLES WEBSTER HAWTHORNE
By the sea
Signed, *circa* 1900–5, 50½in by 36in (128.3cm by 91.4cm)
New York $93,500(£52,235). 4.VI.82

WILLIAM ROBINSON LEIGH
Zuni pottery painter
Signed and dated *1907*, 25in by 30in (63.5cm by 76.2cm)
New York $148,500 (£82,961). 22.X.81

This painting was executed after the artist's first trip to New Mexico, where he had been on an
assignment to paint the Laguna and Zuni Pueblo country for the Santa Fe Railroad Co

WINSLOW HOMER
East Hampton, Long Island
Signed, inscribed with the title and dated *1874*, 10in by 21½in (25.4cm by 54.6cm)
New York $577,500 (£322,626). 22.X.81

JOHN HENRY TWACHTMAN
Winter landscape
Signed, 30in by 30in (76.2cm by 76.2cm)
New York $143,000 (£79,888). 4.VI.82

Opposite
WINSLOW HOMER
Three boys on the shore
Gouache and watercolour on paper laid down on board, twice signed and dated *1873*, 8¼in by 14in
(21cm by 35.5cm)
New York $297,000 (£165,922). 23.IV.82

EDWARD HOPPER
Summer in the city
Signed, 1949, 20in by 30in (50.8cm by 76.2cm)
New York $330,000 (£184,358). 10.XII.81

ANDREW WYETH
Marsh hawk
Tempera on masonite, signed, 1964, 30$\frac{1}{2}$in by 45in (77.5cm by 114.3cm)
New York $462,000 (£258,101). 10.XII.81

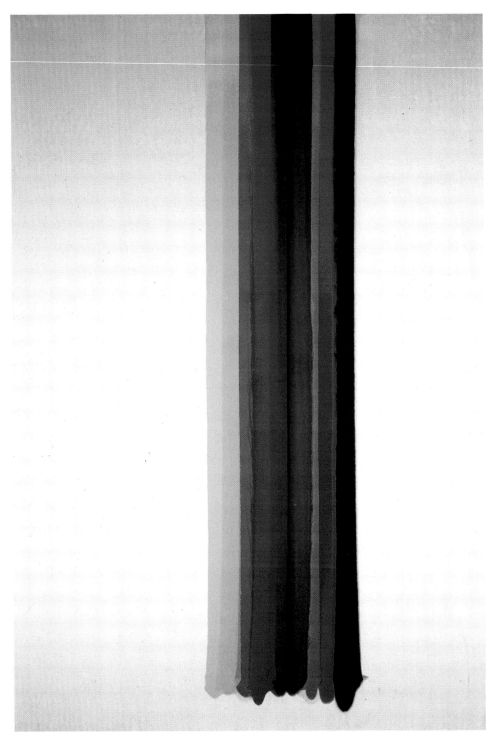

MORRIS LOUIS
Sky opening
Signed, inscribed with the title and dated *'61* on the reverse, 86½in by 59¼in
(219.7cm by 150.5cm)
New York $275,000 (£153,631). 19.XI.81
From the collection of the late Mrs William H. Weintraub

KENNETH NOLAND
Empyrean
Inscribed with the title and dated *1960* on the reverse, 81½in by 81¾in (207cm by 207.6cm)
New York $330,000 (£184,358). 19.XI.81
From the collection of the late Mrs William H. Weintraub

MARK ROTHKO
Untitled (red)
1958, 82$\frac{1}{4}$in by 49in (208.9cm by 124.5cm)
New York $264,000(£147,486). 20.V.82

CY TWOMBLY
Untitled
1968, 68in by 85in (172.7cm by 215.9cm)
New York $192,500 (£107,542). 19.XI.81

RICHARD ESTES
Woolworth's
1974, 38in by 55in (96.5cm by 139.7cm)
New York $143,000 (£79,888). 4.V.82

MALCOLM MORLEY
Safety is your business
Signed, inscribed with the title and dated *71*, 88in by 110¾in (223.6cm by 281.4cm)
London £24,200 ($43,318). 1.VII.82

CHINESE SCHOOL
The waterfront at Canton
Circa 1855, 33½in by 77½in (85.1cm by 196.8cm)
Hong Kong HK $242,000(£23,495:$42,056). 20.V.82

LOUIS BELANGER
A bridge over the Cabarita River, Westmorland parish, Jamaica
One of a group of three views of Jamaica, watercolour over pencil heightened with bodycolour, signed
and dated *1796*, 18½in by 26½in (47cm by 67.3cm)
London £8,800($15,752). 10.II.82

TINUS DE JONGH
Victoria Falls
Signed and dated *1933*, 49⅝in by 61¾in (126cm by 157cm)
Johannesburg R18,000 (£9,326:$16,694). 26.XI.81
From the collection of Mr and Mrs L. Orr

RUFINO TAMAYO
La sonrisa
Signed and dated *0–46*, 49¼in by 108½in (125.1cm by 275.6cm)
New York $275,000(£153,631). 2.XII.81

EMILIO PETTORUTI
Intimidad
Signed and dated *1941*, and signed, inscribed with the title and dated on the reverse,
51¼in by 35in (130.2cm by 88.9cm)
New York $74,250(£41,480). 10.VI.82
From the collection of the Seattle Art Museum, Washington

Prints

ALBRECHT DÜRER
The little courier
Engraving, *circa* 1496, $4\frac{1}{4}$in by 3in (10.8cm by 7.7cm)
£4,950 ($8,861)

Below
DOMENICO DEL BARBIERE
Skeletons and flayed men
Engraving, *circa* 1550, $9\frac{3}{8}$in by $13\frac{1}{8}$in (23.8cm by 33.4cm)
£4,400 ($7,876)

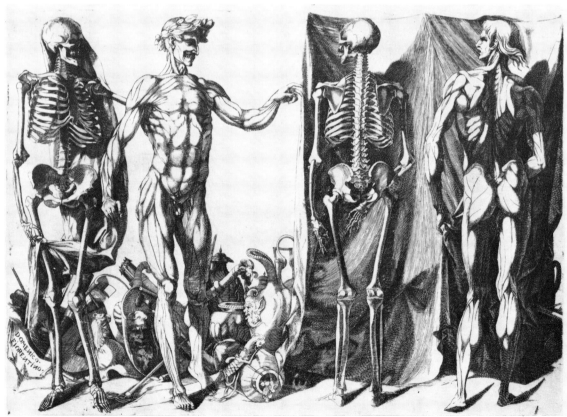

The prints illustrated on this page are from the collection of HSH the Prince Fürstenberg and were sold
in London on 18 June 1982

COLOGNE SCHOOL
St Jerome in penitence
Hand-coloured dotted print, *circa* 1470–80, 10⅛in by 7⅛in (25.7cm by 18cm), bound into a manuscript
copy of the *Meditations on the Passion* attributed to St Bonaventura, *circa* 1480–1500
London £90,200($161,458). 18.VI.82

Thirteen other prints were bound into the volume: a hand-coloured woodcut of *Christ as the Man of
Sorrows*, Netherlandish school, *circa* 1490–1500; and a set of twelve engravings of *The Passion* by
Israhel van Meckenem, first states, *circa* 1470–80

REMBRANDT HARMENSZ. VAN RIJN
The three trees
Etching, drypoint and engraving, 1643, 8¼in by 11in (21.1cm by 28cm)
New York $121,000 (£67,598). 14.XI.81

Opposite
REMBRANDT HARMENSZ. VAN RIJN
Clement de Jonghe, printseller
Etching and drypoint, the first state of six, 1651, 8⅛in by 6⅜in (20.7cm by 16.1cm)
New York $110,000 (£61,453). 14.XI.81

GEORGE STUBBS, ARA
Freeman, keeper to the Earl of Clarendon, with a hound and a wounded doe
Mezzotint, only state, published 16 October 1804, 15½in by 19⅜in (39.5cm by 49.3cm)
London £10,450($18,706). 19.XI.81

This is one of very few impressions of this plate taken during Stubbs's lifetime

Opposite, above
GABRIEL LORY THE ELDER after GERARD DE LA BARTHE
Vue de la Mokavaïa et de la maison de Mr Paschkof à Moscou
One of a group of eleven *Views in and around Moscow*, coloured etchings, published 1799, each
approximately 19¼in by 28⅜in (49cm by 72cm)
London £4,620($8,270). 19.XI.81

Opposite, below
MATTHEW DUBOURG after JAMES POLLARD
Stage coach (The Brighton Comet)
Coloured aquatint, published November 1822, 14⅞in by 16¾in (37.9cm by 42.5cm)
London £1,430($2,560). 19.XI.81

PABLO PICASSO
Femme au fauteuil no 1 (Le manteau polonais)
Lithograph, final state, December 1948–January 1949, 27½in by 21½in (70cm by 54.5cm)
New York $60,500 (£33,799). 13.XI.81
From the collection of the late Anne Burnett Tandy

EMIL NOLDE
Junges paar
Lithograph, signed, inscribed with the title and *In dieser Fassung ein Druck*, 1913, 24½in by 20¼in
(62.4cm by 51.6cm)
London £33,000($59,070). 4.XII.81

Photographs

LADY CLEMENTINA HAWARDEN
Girl at a window
Albumen print, *circa* 1860–64, 3¼in by 2½in (8.4cm by 6.5cm)
London £3,740 ($6,695). 28.X.81

Man seated in a doorway
Calotype, one of an album of ninety-nine calotypes and salt prints, *circa* 1845–55, each approximately
6⅝in by 8¼in (17cm by 21cm)
London £24,200 ($43,318). 25.VI.82

VICTOR REGNAULT
Le parc de St Cloud
Salt print from waxed-paper negative, *circa* 1850–54, $18\frac{7}{8}$in by 15in (48cm by 38cm)
London £8,250($14,768). 12.III.82

EUGENE ATGET
Fête du trône
Gold-toned printing-out paper print, inscribed with the title and with the studio stamp on the reverse, *circa* 1910, approximately 7in by 9½in (17.8cm by 24.1cm)
New York $13,750(£7,682). 24.V.82

Right
HEINRICH KUHN
Child blowing a soap bubble
Gum bichromate print, *circa* 1910, 29¼in by 21⅞in (74.3cm by 55.5cm)
New York $11,550(£6,453). 24.V.82
From the collection of Robert Mapplethorpe

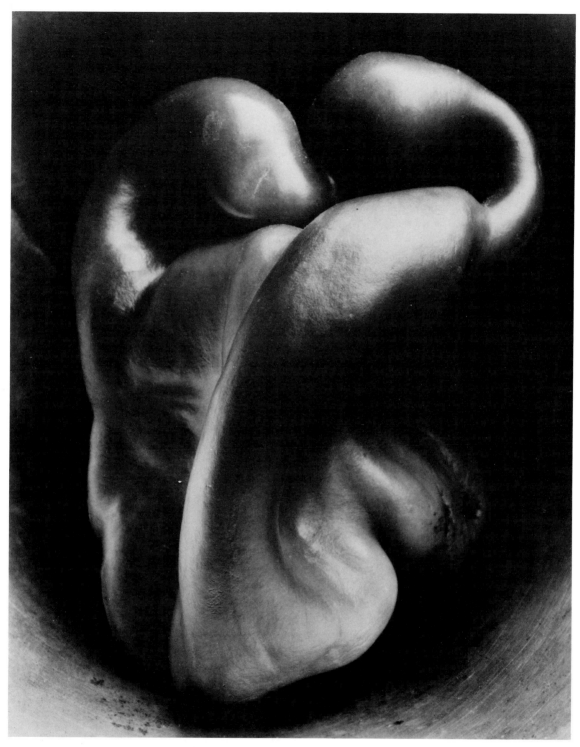

EDWARD WESTON
Pepper no 30
Silver print, signed and dated *1930* on the mount, and signed, dated and with the photographer's
label on the reverse, printed *circa* 1940, 9½in by 7½in (24.1cm by 19cm)
New York $24,200 (£13,520). 25.V.82

Manuscripts and printed books

Tacuinum Sanitatis, a grocer selling raisins, one of 132 miniatures from a manuscript on vellum,
probably Lombardy, early fifteenth century
New York $247,500 (£138,268). 30.X.81
From the collection of the late Carleton R. Richmond

This is the long-lost portion of a manuscript in the Bibliothèque Municipale, Rouen. The text derives
from an eleventh-century Arabic original by Ibn Botlân and deals with means of preserving health

Gouvernement des Princes, Aristotle sending a letter and Hippocrates viewing his portrait, two of twenty-two miniatures from an illuminated manuscript in French on vellum, Bourges, *circa* 1490
London £159,500 ($285,505). 22.VI.82
Now in the Bibliothèque Nationale, Paris

The volume also includes *Le Bréviaire des Nobles* by Alain Chartier and a list, *Les Noms des Roys de France*. The text of the *Gouvernement des Princes*, a guide to the mysteries of life and health, is said to have been sent by Aristotle to Alexander the Great during his conquest of Persia

Manuscripts from the Fürstenberg Library

Christopher de Hamel

The enormous library of the Prince Fürstenberg fills an entire eighteenth-century tower at Donaueschingen. There are about a thousand manuscripts and as many incunabula. The collection includes books of major international significance, such as the greatest manuscript of the *Niebelungenlied*, but almost more impressive are room after room shelved from floor to ceiling with old printed books in contemporary vellum or uncut in their original wrappers. The library is the massive accumulation of a very rich family over many centuries. One looks in vain for evidence of princely bibliophily as such. There are no book plates or armorial bindings, and almost no eighteenth-century red morocco. This was, and still is, principally a working library on a grand scale. Count Wolfgang von Fürstenberg (1465–1509) bought manuscripts when they were new. Count Wratislaus von Fürstenberg (1600–42) furnished his castle of Messkirch with the latest books. Prince Josef Wilhelm Ernst von Fürstenberg (1699–1762) brought the library to Donaueschingen and under his direction the books were catalogued and ordered as a reference collection. In the nineteenth century, the medieval ancestry of the Fürstenberg family appealed to German romantics: the connoisseur and antiquarian, Joseph, Freiherr von Lassberg (1770–1855), was a close friend and adviser. His own collections were purchased *en bloc* in 1853 by Prince Karl Egon III (1820–92) and thus over 11,000 books and medieval manuscripts were added to the prince's already vast accessions of paintings, mineral specimens, shells, stuffed animals, fossils and freaks of natural history.

Early in 1982, Sotheby's was asked to make a selection of manuscripts to form a single sale. This was a fascinating task, as the range of manuscripts extends as widely as any collection in private hands. The twenty lots finally chosen stretched from the fifth to the fifteenth century. Almost certainly, no book sale has ever spanned a thousand years without leaving the Middle Ages. The exceptionally early manuscripts and fragments are one of the surprises and delights of the library at Donaueschingen: even single leaves and binding scraps from before the year 800 are exceedingly scarce. The early manuscripts selected for the sale were only a few of the many at Donaueschingen, and included a complete eighth-century copy of Orosius's *World History* (Fig 1), parts of two Bible manuscripts and a medical text whose eight pages of uncials in black and red formed the oldest secular manuscript known in private hands.

Fig 1 *Opposite*
OROSIUS
World History, a page from a manuscript on vellum, Corbie Abbey, northern France, late eighth century
London £220,000 ($393,800). 21.VI.82
From the collection of HSH the Prince Fürstenberg

Preceptis tuis parui beatissimi pater
Augustine itaque ut inuentem rem efficerem
suasit quiem libens et quiem quiem egrin
uatem uis pietatem piesum ds explicitu
induba; frocenetense cui egesim Tu num uemis
ad iudicium lib dresti uasum nedir quis psc ei
psris persem Egisei uitem soliusel de oliueuice
Si tuem ae udluntie te coniectu q; olsea seu tes
imonium contentus sum. Niem ei inuie quiem.
Unie qui picaris fre milies edomum eum sina mulate
oliuessi qsm ensis ienim ielie icoliumen tu fre milie sis
sei comudsie Nonest tie men ienum tuste posase
mie quib; solis ntie tuste insitum est udluntie snie icolioi
quis psc epiesetus usquei iei leper ingsiniciem quien oiie
oledeiengiee ser muluem soliem disciplinies maiis et psc
tie ctione suspensi oldnee icolpsie egrnoi lizeneuem nutus
ignoue mitientur Hieblientuenim psspisis ieppuritus.
quientum brutis et uellinitor isitentum sie ciometilib;
pspinquientiqs hoeesa discesnese amiete Sequise;
Niem disiessi nenisr intes edomindsi ietq; et piie nesir nondsr
quis insiecientus oisepunt sa| his qusiememens zelietie.
Frie mienqs oliminum ieedomu nonquiesi et uietuiste iepi
torpisi uigilient. Sei et ionseiongie soll; iei iem drisi nieli
zelient. Unie sie ium mistieiusier siem bniei inoiuengelius

A fifth-century Bible fragment is particularly intriguing (Fig 2). No older Western manuscript is ever recorded to have been sold. Other scraps from the same manuscript are known, the largest being in the Landesbibliotheks at Fulda and Stuttgart. The text here is from Ezechiel and the whole volume must originally have comprised the six Major Prophets. The Donaueschingen pieces were recovered in 1909 and 1920 from inside the back of a medieval bookbinding, which had been purchased by Lassberg from Constance Cathedral. In 1343, the inventory of Constance recorded the presence there of a volume of six biblical books (this sounds like the Major Prophets) of great antiquity, 'Item VI libri biblie in uno volumine de litera multum antiqua', which may well have been the book cut up soon afterwards by the cathedral binder. It had probably become unreadable. More tantalizing is the fact that many of the oldest Constance books had earlier been brought from the great abbey of Reichenau, on an island in Lake Constance. During the abbacy of Erlebald (823–38), the monks there recorded a 'Liber prophetarum quem Hiltiger de Italia adduxit' ('a volume of the Prophets [rare enough in any case] which Hiltiger had brought from Italy'). Since our manuscript was certainly written in Italy, it is likely that we know every owner it has had since the ninth century.

Another manuscript which can be identified with a medieval description is the thirteenth-century illuminated Bible, signed twice by its scribe, Cambius of Vicenza. The manuscript has many textual corrections, and long notes explaining that these emendations were made in accordance with the Carthusian General Chapters of 1416–17 and 1431. On one page in the middle, as if deliberately concealed, is the medieval ownership inscription of the famous Carthusian abbey near Erfurt. The late fifteenth-century catalogue of that monastery recorded two Bibles 'emendata in Carthusia' – the present manuscript and a Gutenburg Bible – into which the corrections were transferred. The monastery was suppressed in 1803. The Gutenburg copy is not known to have survived, although several extant copies are in Erfurt bindings. The manuscript Bible was acquired from a bookseller in Stuttgart in 1819 and so came eventually to Donaueschingen.

The library does not own a Gutenburg Bible, although it has a fine block-book and a great many books printed before 1500. Two manuscripts belong to the transitional period before printing took over. One is a little fifteenth-century manuscript prayer-book, illustrated with contemporary woodcuts. The second was among the books selected for the sale and aroused a surprising amount of public curiosity. It is a northern Dutch Book of Hours, with twelve full-page miniatures painted circa 1430. About a dozen closely related manuscripts are known from the same workshop and they have a feature in common. The pictures are stamped in the outer margins with pale-red, printed letters. This curious way in which individual painters marked their work is not known to have been used in any other European workshop. The Donaueschingen manuscript is marked with a printed gothic letter 'b'. The point of particular interest is that there are some reasons for assigning the workshop to Haarlem. One of the oldest and most discredited bibliographical legends is that printing was not invented by Gutenburg in Mainz, circa 1450 – as is universally accepted now – but in the town of Haarlem, circa 1430. It can only be a matter of conjecture, but it seems likely that the famous legend derives from the use of printed

Fig 2
A fragment from the *Book of Ezechiel*, on vellum, northern Italy, fifth century
London £17,600 ($31,504). 21.VI.82
From the collection of HSH the Prince Fürstenberg

letters like those here. So it may be that the notorious old story contains an element of truth after all.

The illuminated manuscripts at Donaueschingen vary a great deal in quality. There are a number of Books of Hours (mostly imperfect), but none of the richly decorated Missals and Antiphoners with which more recent collections are stocked. Some of the vernacular romances are profusely illustrated, but often with the roughly coloured drawings so characteristic of secular manuscripts. Ultimately, all the best pictorial art of the Middle Ages was ecclesiastical, despite a few outstanding exceptions.

One manuscript with most unusual decoration is an early eleventh-century Sacramentary. The calendar points clearly to the cathedral of Augsburg and the book was possibly one of the two golden Missals ('*missalia deaurata*') recorded there *circa* 1096. Every page of the manuscript has great initials in burnished gold and there are several full-page interlaced letters on deep-purple grounds. There are two further full-page miniatures (*cf* Fig 3) and two large uncoloured drawings, executed in the finest style of Ottonian art. The closest parallels are with a manuscript life of St Ulrich of Augsburg, now in the National Library, Vienna, prepared by Abbot Bruno of Reichenau (1008–48) for Abbot Fridebold of Augsburg. Eleventh-century manuscripts are rare in private hands; richly illuminated examples are almost unknown.

One of a number of interesting twelfth-century manuscripts at Donaueschingen was a Collectarius, or book of collects, written for a bishop in the middle years of the century. Like the fifth-century fragments, the manuscript belonged to Constance Cathedral and it was still there when it was bought by Lassberg sometime before 1824. The Bishop of Constance from 1138 to 1166 was Hermann of Arbon, and the book was probably made for his personal use. It includes prayers and benedictions for many occasions. One remarkable series comprises prayers for a king, for a king in council, for the successful outcome of a council and for victory over the king's enemies. Intriguingly, the king is addressed in the second person, '*tu*', which implies that he was actually present when the prayers were to be spoken. The occasion may well have been the Diet of Constance in 1153. In that year, the newly elected king, Frederick Barbarossa, met the papal envoys in council there. Events culminated in the Treaty of Constance on 23 March, whereby Frederick agreed not to make peace with the Pope's enemies and the Pope agreed to crown Frederick as Holy Roman Emperor. In some ways, this bulky little manuscript epitomizes the Donaueschingen Collection. It is an unassuming volume in its plain medieval binding, yet it has been in only two collections since it was written in the twelfth century, and it is quite possible that it was last used by Bishop Hermann in the late winter of 1153, in Constance Cathedral, in the presence of half the papal curia, for the benediction of the warrior king, Frederick Barbarossa. It is an emotive relic of great interest, and a pleasing item to find on the shelf of a private library.

Fig 3 *Opposite*
Sacramentary, the Crucifixion, a miniature from an illuminated manuscript on vellum, Augsburg Cathedral, early eleventh century
London £308,000 ($551,320). 21.VI.82
From the collection of HSH the Prince Fürstenberg

Gospels of St Luke and St John, a page from a manuscript on vellum, Exeter Cathedral, late eleventh century
London £11,000($19,690). 22.VI.82
From the collection of the late Dr A. N. L. Munby; and now in the Bodleian Library, Oxford

This manuscript was probably written in the scriptorium established by Leofric, Bishop of Exeter (1046–72), and is listed in the cathedral inventory of 1506

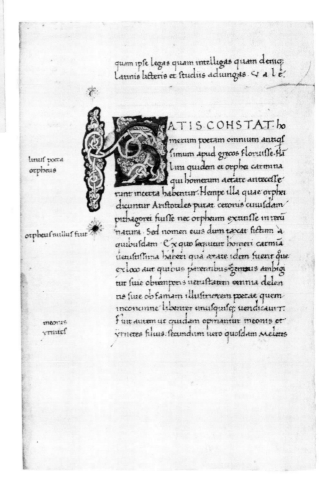

HERCULES BRUNUS
De Gestis Romanorum and other texts, a page from an illuminated manuscript on vellum, Florence, *circa* 1460–75
London £2,640($4,726). 8.XII.81
From the collection of K. H. Rogers FSA

This volume was formerly in the collections of Dr Anthony Askew (sold at Sotheby's in 1784 for 16s), Michael Wodhull (sold at Sotheby's in 1803 for 6s 6d), Richard Heber (sold at Evans's in 1836 for 10s), Sir Thomas Phillipps (sold at Sotheby's in 1899 for 14s and resold at Sotheby's in 1903 for 27s), Sir Sydney Cockerell, Ethel May Offer and Richard Emery Sandell

RUNGIA RAJU
An album of fifty-two botanical watercolours, Madras, *circa* 1884–86
London £18,700 ($33,473). 29.III.82

This is one of three albums by Rungia Raju made for the Governor of Madras, Mountstuart Elphinstone Grant Duff, who was a distinguished botanist and an expert on the flora of India

The 'first' *Rasamanjari* series

Mark Zebrowski

The illustrations to the 'first' *Rasamanjari* series, painted at Basohli in the Himalayan foothills, are among the most important and exquisite Indian paintings to have survived. The page which sold this season was therefore among the most significant items in a major Indian sale held to coincide with the Festival of India.

The Pahari, or Hill kingdoms, among which Basohli was a state of some importance, were ruled by Hindu Rajput kings, feudatories of the Muslim Mughal emperors of Delhi. Yet, whereas Mughal art is realistic and restrained, and Rajput painting in Rajasthan, nearer the Mughal capital, combines Islamic and Hindu sensibilities, the isolated Hill schools gained potency and fire only from each other. Closed to the sober realism of the Plains, seventeenth-century Pahari pictures often have a concentrated energy which belies their small size.

Until the mid seventeenth century, no painting seems to have been patronized by any Hill raja, although it was already in full flower at the Mughal and Rajasthani courts. The Basohli rajas had traditionally been ardent devotees of the god Shiva but, during mid century, Vaishnavism, worship of the god Vishnu and his incarnations Krishna and Rama, gained the tacit support of Raja Sangram Pal (1635–*circa* 1673) and his successor. Painting bursts forth during their reigns, and it is likely that the impulse behind it was the recent arrival of Vaishnavism. Both kings were interested in secular literature and one of the most popular works was the *Rasamanjari*, a long poem describing the moods and activities of ideal lovers, written by Bhanu Datta in the fourteenth century. The heroes and heroines of such poems came to be associated with Krishna and Radha, whose amorous exploits were a source of delight to Vaishnava devotees. So when the *Rasamanjari* was first illustrated at Basohli, in this series, probably through the patronage of Sangram Pal, the hero is shown as Krishna with his blue complexion, staff, flute and peacock-feather crown. Although earlier illustrations to the *Rasamanjari* were done in Rajasthan, this has been identified by W. G. Archer, as the 'first' of three series painted at Basohli between 1660 and 1695.

One page depicts the heroine, or *nayika*, relating amorous disappointments to a confidante, while the hero, or *nayaka*, remorsefully beckons outside (Fig 1). The artist has given the *nayika* marvellously expressive gestures. Her abundant jewellery is made of beetle-wing cases pasted onto the page, which glimmer like the emeralds they represent. Even more moving is her confidante's expression of silent compassion. Another page, sold last year, depicts the heroine talking to her paramour at the gate of her house, while her husband tends his cattle in the background (Fig 2). She can be boldly flirtatious, because only her blind and deaf sisters-in-law are at home!

Fig 1
Nateka anabhoga: A disappointed nayika consoled by a female confidante, an Indian miniature from the *Rasamanjari*, Basohli, *circa* 1660–70
London £17,600 ($31,504). 29.III.82

Fig 2
Mudita parakiya nayika: An excited wife greeting Krishna, an Indian miniature from the *Rasamanjari*, Basohli, *circa* 1660–70
London £27,500. 28.IV.81

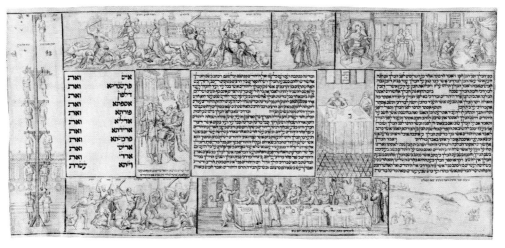

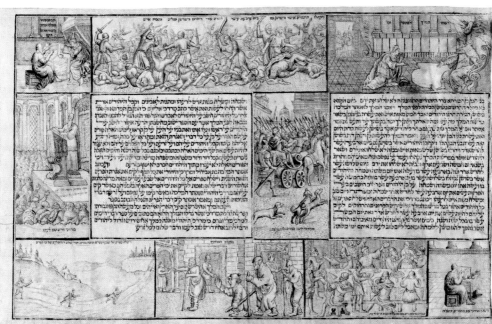

Megillat Esther (*The Scroll of Esther for the Festival of Purim*), an illustrated Hebrew scroll in ashkenazi script on vellum, Holland, *circa* 1620–40
London £66,000 ($118,140). 21.IV.82
From the collection of the Athenaeum, Liverpool

The Bible, scenes from the life of Jonah, four of forty-three miniatures from an
illuminated manuscript in Armenian on vellum, probably New Julfa, Isfahan,
dated *1651* and 1661
London £28,600($51,194). 27.IV.82

A Mamluk *Qur'an*

David James

The *Qur'an* which sold at Sotheby's in April is among the largest in existence. The date and circumstances of production are clear from the manuscript itself. The certificate of commissioning (Fig 1) names the Mamluk patron: 'This glorious, sanctified, revered and noble *Qur'an* is copied by order of our lord the sultan, the possessor, Al-Malik al-Ashraf Abu'l-Nasr Qayt-Bay, May God make him triumphant and grant him definitive victory and extend to him His grace in this world and the next and grant him hope and consolation through Muhammad and his house, Amen.' The colophon gives the name of the scribe, Tenem al-Najmi al-Maliki al-Ashrafi, and the date of completion of the manuscript, 21 Jumada I 894/ 19 April 1489.

Qayt-Bay (1468–96) was undoubtedly the most able of the Circassian, or Burji Mamluk rulers of Egypt (1382–1517). Apart from Al-Nasir Muhammad, the great fourteenth-century ruler, no Mamluk sultan survived for longer than he. Long his reign may have been, but tranquil it was not. Although the sultan did his best to encourage trade with the outside world and organize his affairs at home, he had serious financial, political and military problems which were compounded, and to some extent created, by his relations with the Aq Qoyunlu Turkmans, Uzun Hasan and Ya'qub Bey. Even more ominous for the future of the Mamluks were his dealings with the Ottomans, whose rising military power threatened all of the eastern Mediterranean. To finance his military campaigns against these rivals, the sultan was forced to extort money on a massive scale from his subjects, as well as imposing, probably reluctantly, heavy taxes on trade and commerce. More money was swallowed up by his extensive building programme, including the monument for which he is best remembered, the beautiful mosque-mausoleum outside Cairo (Fig 2).

Although illustrated Mamluk manuscripts are relatively rare, particularly from the Circassian period, a great many beautifully written and illuminated *Qur'ans*, religious poems and prayerbooks survive. Qayt-Bay and several members of his court, notably the emir Yashbak al-Dawadar, were considerable patrons of manuscript production. There are numerous superb copies of the *Qasidat al-Burdah* (*Poem of the Prophet's Mantle*) by Al-Busiri, known to have been made for the sultan. One of these, in the Chester Beatty Library, must rank as the finest manuscript of his reign.[1]

It is therefore surprising that so few *Qur'ans* appear to have been commissioned by Qayt-Bay: no more than a handful survive in Cairo, Dublin and Istanbul. The first

[1] Ms 4168

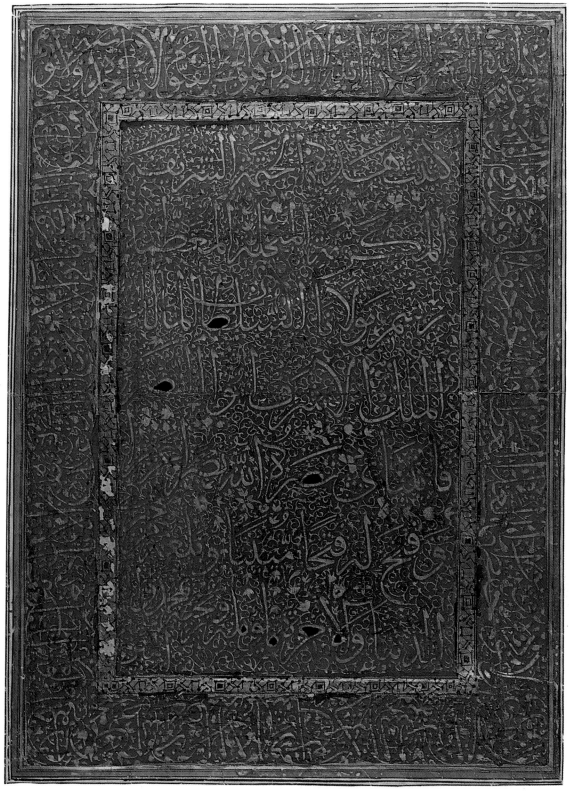

Fig 1
The Qur'an, the certificate of commissioning in *thuluth* script, a page from a Mamluk illuminated Arabic manuscript, copied by Tenem al-Najmi, Egypt, dated 1489, $26\frac{1}{4}$in by $18\frac{3}{8}$in (66.7cm by 46.7cm)
London £88,000($157,520). 26.IV.82
From the collection of the Hagop Kevorkian Fund

Fig 2
FRANCIS FRITH
The mosque of Kaitbey
Albumen print, signed and dated *1858* in the negative, with the title printed on the mount,
15⅜in by 18¼in (39.1cm by 46.5cm)
London £198 ($354). 12.III.82

thirty years of Circassian rule had probably seen the production of the finest examples, which to a large extent perpetuated the tradition of the previous Bahri period
(1250–1390): the highpoint in *Qur'an* illumination had then been the reign of Sultan
Sha'ban (1363–76). By the time of Qayt-Bay, the end of the tradition was in sight.

The copies of the *Qasidah* and the surviving *Qur'ans* show that the art of calligraphy continued to thrive. Calligraphers considered themselves heirs to a long
tradition and looked for their models to the masters of the past. Muhammad bin
Hasan al-Tibi, who lived during the reigns of Qayt-Bay and Qansuh al-Ghuri, composed two examplars of calligraphy.[2] In these, he followed the canons of proportion
laid down by Ibn al-Bawwab four centuries previously. In the *Jami' Mahasin Kitabat
al-Kuttab* (*The Calligrapher's Compendium*), he shows seventeen styles of calligraphy,

[2] One has been published in facsimile. See Muhammad bin Hasan al-Tibi *The Kinds of Arabic
Calligraphy according to the Method of Ibn al-Bawwab* ed Al-Munajjid (Beirut, 1962)

Fig 3

The Qur'an, the colophon in *naskh* and *thuluth* script, a page from a Mamluk illuminated Arabic
manuscript, copied by Tenem al-Najmi, Egypt, dated 1489, $26\frac{1}{4}$ in by $18\frac{3}{8}$ in (66.7cm by 46.7cm)
London £88,000 ($157,520). 26.IV.82
From the collection of the Hagop Kevorkian Fund

all in the manner of Ibn al-Bawwab. Most of them can be recognized in fifteenth-century manuscripts. Many *Qur'ans* and other works were copied in what Al-Tibi calls *naskh faddah*, a variety of *naskh* embodying some of the flattened characteristics of *muhaqqaq* script. This is similar, though not identical, to the script of the *Qur'an* under discussion, which is rounder and less formal.

The scribe of our *Qur'an*, Tenem al-Najmi, was a member of the *Khassakiyah* or royal bodyguard of the sultan. In the chronicle of Muhammad bin Tulun (1473–1546), we are informed that in the year 1499, just after the end of Qayt-Bay's reign, Tenem al-Najmi and Timraz al-Zardkash were sent to Syria to dismiss the Governor of Damascus and appoint the Governor of Aleppo in his place. It seems probable that Tenem was also a member of the royal bodyguard when this *Qur'an* was copied. If so, he was a member of an élite group. The size of the bodyguard underwent great changes from time to time but, according to the Mamluk chronicler, Ibn Iyas, it numbered no more than forty in 1486.

Tenem must have been copying out the manuscript on the instructions of his master and was, no doubt, a man of some cultivation, since the calligraphy is of the highest order. It has a precision which could only have been attained with constant practice, by someone used to copying out documents.

Several styles of illumination seem to have coexisted in Cairo at this time. One is represented by a manuscript in the Chester Beatty Library, which appears to be the work of a foreign, perhaps Turkman painter.[3] This artist illuminated a princely almanac in the same library,[4] for Qayt-Bay, and the copy of the *Iskandername* in Istanbul University Library,[5] for Sultan Timurbugha (1468), Qayt-Bay's short-lived predecessor. He is one of several foreign artists whose activities for the later Circassian Mamluks are still not fully examined. Another style continued in a debased form the tradition of the early part of the century with some Timurid influence.[6]

Our *Qur'an* belongs to the second category, but with some peculiarities of its own. The certificate of commissioning on the opening page is written in gold *riqa*ᶜ over golden sprays and arabesques on a blue ground. Around it is a simple interlace border and, in the outer border running around the central rectangle, is the *Ayat al-Kursi* (*Throne Verse*. II *Al-Baqarah*: 225), which was sometimes used for this purpose. The opening pages of text are in gold *naskh* outlined in black. Above and below are panels giving the *surah* titles and verse counts. At each side are vertical panels with gold sprays of flowers. The ground beneath the text differs somewhat from one page to another – a common enough feature in Mamluk *Qur'ans*. The colophon (Fig 3) is decorated with a large rectangular panel bearing a benediction on the Prophet, contained in an irregular medallion on a ground of gold sprays and fragmentary arabesques over blue. Panels of this type occur in late Mamluk manuscripts, particularly *Qur'ans*. Another example can be seen in the Chester Beatty Qayt-Bay *Qur'an*.

Our manuscript is a fine example of late Mamluk calligraphy and illumination. It is also one of the few Circassian Mamluk *Qur'ans* copied by a person identifiable from historical sources.

---

[3] Ms 1508

[4] Ms 441

[5] Ms 106

[6] See Moritz, B. *Arabic Palaeography* (Cairo, 1905), pl 80

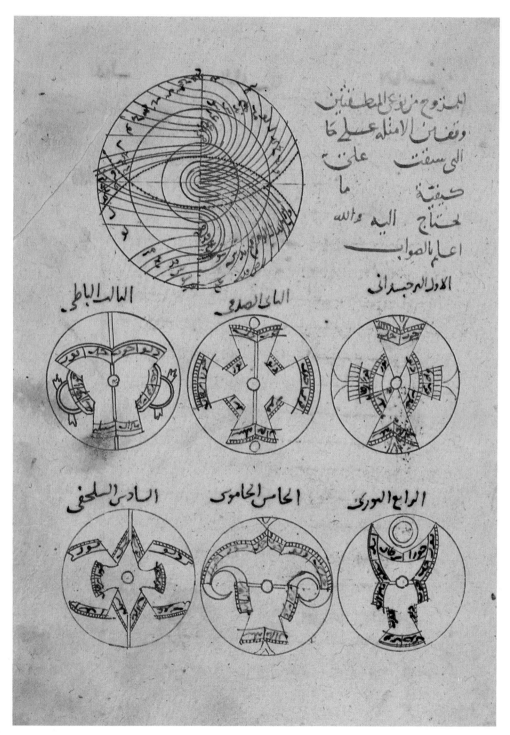

ABU RAYHAN MUHAMMAD BIN AHMAD AL-BIRUNI
Treatise on the Astrolabe, a Seljuk illustrated Arabic manuscript in *naskh* script, copied by
Mahmud bin Muhammad bin Mahmud bin Muhammad al-Mushi, Sivas, Turkey, dated 1231
London £77,000 ($137,830). 27.IV.82

This is one of the earliest known extant copies of the treatise by Al-Biruni (973–*circa* 1050),
bound with three other treatises on the construction, use and theory of the astrolabe, dated
1231, 1238 and *circa* 1238

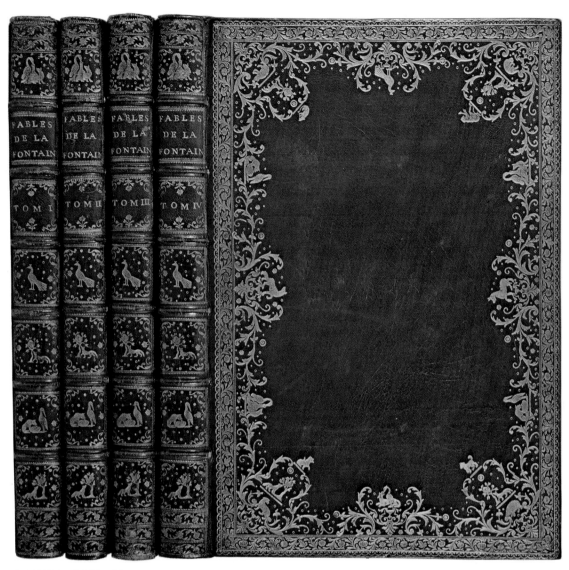

JEAN DE LA FONTAINE
Fables choisies, four volumes, with frontispiece and 275 engraved plates after Jean-Baptiste Oudry,
bound in red morocco with gilt tooling by Louis Douceur, Desaint & Saillant et Durand, Paris, 1755–59
Monte Carlo FF233,100 (£21,268 : $38,070). 10.II.82
From the collection of the Greffulhe family

This is one of two or three copies especially executed by Louis Douceur, who was binder to Louis XV

Opposite
ANDREAS VESALIUS
De humani corporis fabrica libri septem, first edition, Johannes Oporinus, Basel, 1543
New York $22,000 (£12,291). 5.V.82
From the collection of Dr Crawford W. Adams

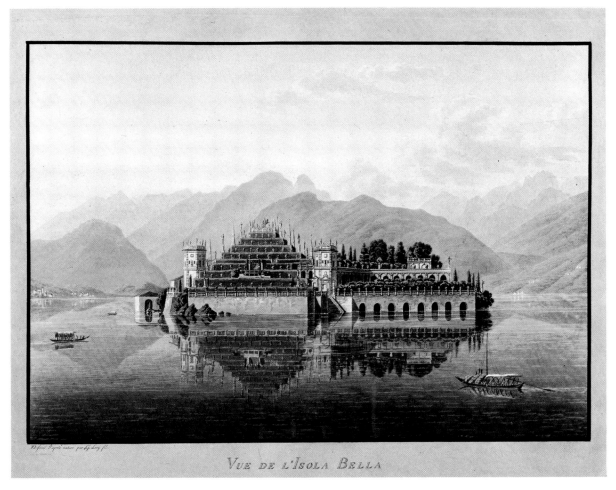

VUE DE L'ISOLA BELLA

GABRIEL LORY THE YOUNGER
Voyage pittoresque de Genève à Milan par le Simplon, first edition, thirty-five hand-coloured aquatinted plates, extra-illustrated with six watercolours, bound in maroon morocco by Simier, Paris, 1811
London £25,300 ($45,287). 16.XI.81

Opposite
JOHN GOULD
The Birds of Australia, eight volumes, 681 hand-coloured lithographed plates after J. & E. Gould and H. C. Richter, 1848–69
London £35,200 ($63,008). 6.IV.82

DACELO CERVINA: Gould

DAVID JONES
One of a set of ten proof impressions of wood-engraved
illustrations to *The Chester Play of the Deluge*, signed
and dated *'27*
London £1,078($1,930). 9.XI.81

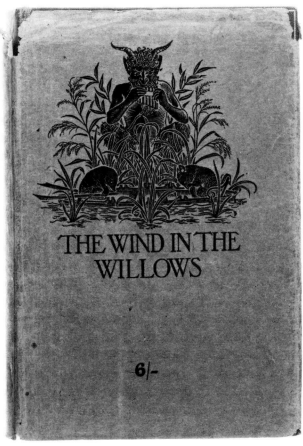

KENNETH GRAHAME
The Wind in the Willows, first edition with original dust
jacket, presentation copy with autograph inscription to
Constance Smedley, 1908
London £3,520($6,301). 12.X.81

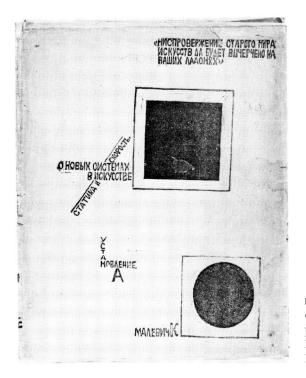

KASIMIR MALEVICH
O novykh sistemakh v iskusstve (*On new Systems in Art*), three
plates and illustrations by the author, wrappers by El
Lissitzky, Artel of Artistic Work, Vitebsk, 1919
London £3,080($5,513). 24.XI.81

KAY NIELSEN
Minon-Minette, an ink and watercolour drawing heightened
with gold to illustrate *In Powder and Crinoline*, signed and
dated '12
London £5,280 ($9,451). 21.VII.82

HEINRICH HOFFMANN
Lustige Geschichten und drollige Bilder (*Struwwelpeter*),
first edition, with hand-coloured lithographed
illustrations by the author, Literarische Anstalt,
Frankfurt-am-Main, 1845
London £13,200 ($23,628). 2.VI.82

EDWARD LEAR
A Book of Nonsense, an album of
fifty-three autograph limericks
illustrated with pen and ink
drawings
London £17,600 ($31,504).
14.X.81

This set of drawings is one of
several produced by Lear for
friends after publication of the
first edition of *A Book of Nonsense*
in 1846. It incorporates twenty
new verses which were
subsequently used in the
enlarged edition of 1862

WILLIAM HENRY IRELAND
A love letter from Shakespeare to Anne Hathaway, one of an album of Shakespearian forgeries
compiled by Ireland in 1805 for presentation to the Prince of Wales, on Elizabethan paper
London £13,200 ($23,628). 30.VI.82

From 1794 to 1796 William Ireland convinced scholars that he had discovered a cache of
autograph manuscripts and papers belonging to Shakespeare. His forgeries were exposed but he
successfully exploited the notoriety, and in a preface to this album he explains his intention to
send copies of his work to 'the leading persons who had subscribed to a belief in their authenticity'

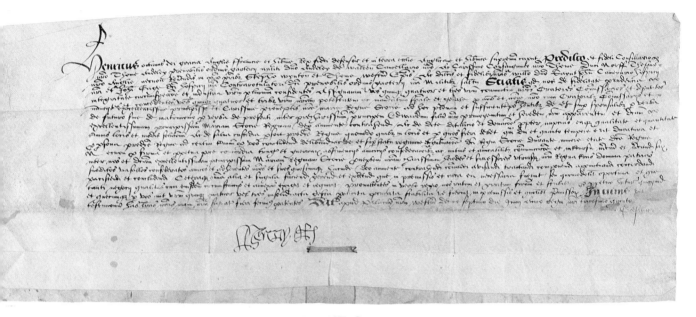

HENRY VIII
A signed document appointing
commissioners to treat for the betrothal of
Prince Edward and Mary Queen of Scots, on
vellum, with the Great Seal of England,
Westminster, 27 June 1543
London £18,700 ($33,473). 17.XII.81

After defeating the Scots at the Battle of
Solway Moss, 14 December 1542, Henry VIII
applied heavy pressure to secure a marriage
between his son Edward, aged six, and Mary
Stuart, then in her first year

Left
LUDWIG VAN BEETHOVEN
An autograph transcript of part of the finale
to Act 1 of Mozart's *Don Giovanni*, nineteen
pages, *circa* 1804–6
London £33,000 ($59,070). 14.IV.82

This manuscript was formerly owned by
Mendelssohn and bears a presentation
inscription by him to Liszt

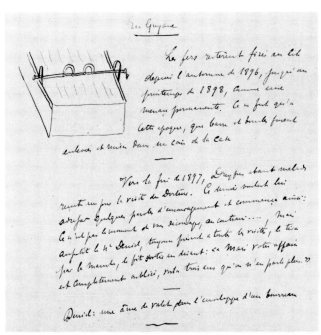

THE DREYFUS CASE
A group of some 170 letters and papers by or relating
to central figures in the case, much of it from the files
of Alfred Dreyfus's lawyer Maître Labori, and used by
him in the trial at Rennes
New York $27,500 (£15,363). 6.IV.82

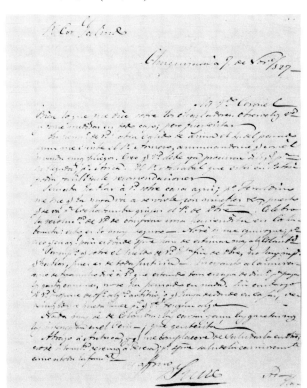

ANTONIO JOSE DE SUCRE
A group of 102 letters to Colonel León Galindo, concerning
the problems of Sucre's presidency of Bolivia, 24 April
1826–12 April 1828
New York $93,500 (£52,235). 3.XII.81

JOHN QUINCY ADAMS
An autograph letter probably to Dr Benjamin Rush,
concerning Jefferson and foreign policy, 10 October
and 19 December 1808
New York $8,800 (£4,916). 28.IV.82

Left

MARIE ANTOINETTE

Autograph instructions to the Duchesse de Tourzel, newly appointed governess to the royal children, describing the Dauphin's character, written eleven days after the storming of the Bastille, 25 July 1789

London £10,780($19,296). 11.XI.81

Right

VINCENT VAN GOGH

An autograph letter in English to the painter Horace Levens, containing a statement of his artistic aims after contact with Impressionism and the Post-Impressionists, Paris, 1886

London £15,950($28,551). 15.IV.82

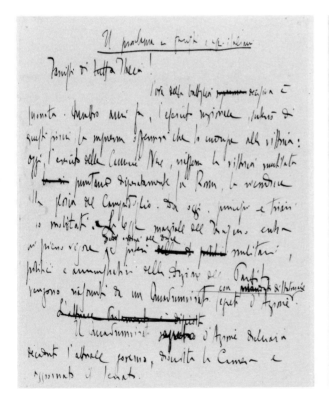

BENITO MUSSOLINI

The autograph draft of his 'proclamation of revolution', announcing the Fascist seizure of power, issued in the name of the Quadrumvirato on the evening before the March on Rome, October 1922

London £12,100($21,659). 15.IV.82

JANE AUSTEN

An autograph letter to her sister Cassandra, giving an account of her life in Bath, 8–11 April 1805

London £11,000($19,690). 30.VI.82

Wagner letters

David R. Murray

Richard Wagner was an indefatigable letter writer. Some musicians are content to communicate solely through their works, but for Wagner communication, whether of artistic ideas, daily needs or transcendental visions, was the very stuff of life, spilling over into every facet of his being. The series of overwhelming music dramas form the core of Wagner's legacy to future generations, but there are also the prose writings, large in number and extremely diverse in subject matter, his daily conversations on art and life, faithfully chronicled in the diaries of his wife, Cosima, and finally his voluminous correspondence.

From a letter addressed to Ludwig II of Bavaria in 1869, it seems that Wagner liked to devote himself to letters two or three times a day. This would certainly account for their extraordinary number, so great in fact that the complete edition of Wagner's letters will run to a projected fifteen volumes. The importance of Wagner's letters was realized at an early date and they began to appear in print in the late 1880s, only a few years after the composer's death. Most of these publications are devoted to Wagner's exchanges with one particular correspondent and many print the letters with incomplete and corrupt texts – hence the need for a complete critical edition, though this venture is still in its early stages.

All these factors add to the stature of the present group of letters by Wagner and his circle, which is remarkable both for its scope and content (Fig 1). It consists of around 400 letters and manuscripts, with contributions from most of the main figures in the Wagner story: Ludwig II (Fig 2), Nietzsche, Hans von Bülow, Hans Richter, Mathilde Wesendonk and the composer's two wives, Minna and Cosima. Not all of these were written to Wagner, but they concern his life, personality and works. The real treasure of this collection, however, is a series of 167 letters by the composer himself, over ninety of which are unpublished or published in incomplete and inaccurate versions. These cover the whole of Wagner's career, beginning in 1837, when he was twenty-four years old, and continuing until a month before his death in 1883.

There is a great deal of material here about early performances of Wagner's operas, particularly *Tannhäuser* in Paris in 1861, and about the growth of his artistic projects, both musical and literary. Sometimes Wagner offers directions for the performance of his works, pointing out sections which will need special attention in rehearsal; for example, his letter of 28 October 1852 to the musical director of the opera house at Schwerin about *Lohengrin*. Other letters detail his reactions to performances and his

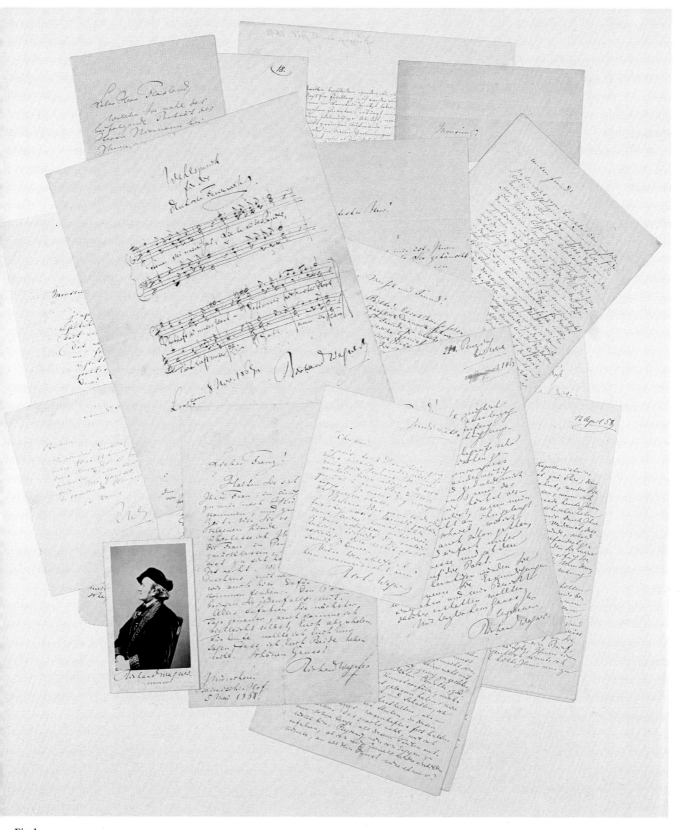

Fig 1
A selection from a group of some 400 letters and manuscripts relating to the life and work of Richard Wagner
London total £129,991 ($232,684). 14/15.IV.82

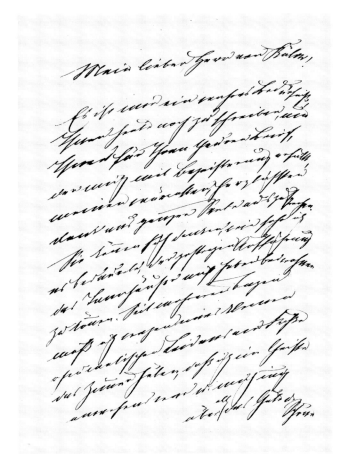

Fig 2
LUDWIG II
An autograph letter to Hans von Bülow, about *Tannhäuser*
and *Das Rheingold*, 26 February 1869
London £5,720 ($10,239). 15.IV.82

Fig 3
RICHARD WAGNER
An autograph letter to his niece, Johanna Wagner,
about *Tannhäuser* and *The Ring*, Zurich, 3 June 1857
London £2,090 ($3,741). 14.IV.82

negotiations with various theatre authorities. There are a number of important letters
to singers, including Josef Tichatschek (the first Rienzi and the first Tannhäuser),
Emil Scaria (one of the first interpreters of Wotan) and Gustav Siehr (the first Hagen
in *Götterdämmerung*, and one of the first singers of Gurnemanz in *Parsifal*). In these
letters, Wagner tells us something of his own view of the rôles he created: for instance,
in a letter to Gustav Siehr, written a fortnight after the first Bayreuth Festival, he
remarks that he never had a baritone voice in mind for Wotan, despite its high
tessitura; instead, he wanted a true bass, but with a wide range. He even hints that
he might alter some of the high notes, to encourage basses to consider the part. The
most revealing of these letters, however, are the three addressed to Wagner's niece,
Johanna. Wagner had high hopes for Johanna: she was a fine actress as well as a good
singer and a successful interpreter of the rôles of Elisabeth (*Tannhäuser*) and Ortrud
(*Lohengrin*). In the late 1850s, however, her father, Wagner's brother Albert, persuaded
Johanna to take on more lucrative rôles, rather than specializing in Wagnerian parts.

In a long letter of 3 June 1857 (Fig 3), Wagner tells Johanna of his disappointment in her: he had hoped that she might become the chief exponent of his female rôles and even had her in mind for Brünnhilde in *The Ring*. Instead, he writes: 'I see that you are treading the familiar path of a future "prima donna".'

Wagner's personality is normally portrayed in grey, if not black, terms. He certainly expected a great deal of his friends, yet Wagner did much to support those people he considered gifted. He was particularly concerned with the career of Hans von Bülow, whose wife he was later to marry. Von Bülow's mother wished her son to pursue a career in law, and Wagner wrote to her pleading that Hans might be allowed to develop his considerable musical gifts.

One of the highlights of this collection is an unpublished letter to Franz Liszt, dated 12 April 1853. The letter in question is another in support of a young musician – not von Bülow this time, but Gustav Schöneck, a conductor and a pupil of Wagner's. Schöneck had studied *Der fliegende Holländer* with Wagner and now wished to mount a production of *Tannhäuser* at the Kroll Theater in Berlin. Wagner was very impressed with the young man and wrote enthusiastically to Liszt about the Berlin project. At this time, Wagner was a political exile from Germany; Liszt, as court conductor at Weimar, could therefore do much more to further Schöneck's plans. Liszt is not mentioned by name in this letter, but it is obvious from the affectionate tone and Liszt's reply that he is indeed the recipient.

There is also a series of fourteen letters to Princess Carolyne Sayn-Wittgenstein, Liszt's mistress. These date from the mid 1850s and contain material of great interest, particularly with regard to Wagner's progress with the composition of *The Ring*. One apparently unpublished letter is concerned with the philosophy of Schopenhauer, and gives news of Wagner's work on *Siegfried*. Two letters to Princess Sayn-Wittgenstein date from a crucial period in Wagner's life – the spring of 1858, when his affair with Mathilde Wesendonk came to a head and precipitated a crisis in his marriage. The first of these letters dates from just five days after the composer's wife, Minna, had intercepted a note between the two lovers. In many ways it is an escape from the turmoil that surrounded him, a discourse about music's position *vis-à-vis* the other arts and an appreciation of the Spanish playwright, Calderón. Wagner also mentions his work on *Tristan* and the fact that Minna has gone to Brestenberg to receive treatment for her heart ailment. The letter is long, running to some ten pages; its successor is shorter, but touches on the delicate emotional situation in Zurich and the fact that Wagner now found the atmosphere there unbearably claustrophobic. Later that same year Wagner and Minna separated, though the composer kept in touch by letter during the next few years. One of these letters, apparently unpublished, is found in the present collection.

Wagner's letters offer insights not only into his own music, but also into that of other men. His tastes were catholic and stretched far beyond the art of his own day. He made an edition of Palestrina's *Stabat Mater* and was a fervent admirer of Bach's '48', from which he would often play at the piano. One of the letters in this group discusses Bach's motet *Singet dem Herrn ein neues Lied*, BWV 225: Wagner thought that Bach's long melismas in his word-setting could be improved upon, and provided a musical example to illustrate his argument. Wagner was a distinguished conductor of

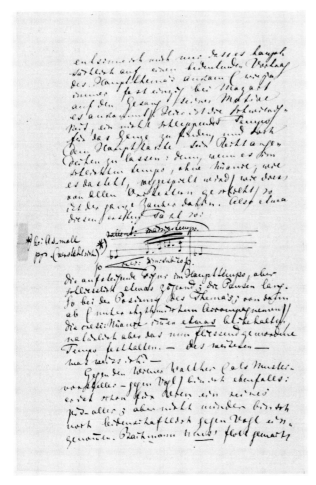

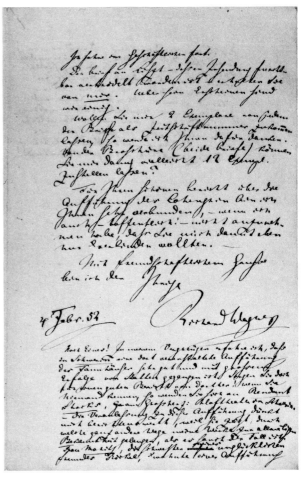

Fig 4
RICHARD WAGNER
An autograph letter to Hans von Bülow, about
Mozart's Symphony no 39 in E flat major, K 543,
Tribschen, 13 March 1868
London £2,750 ($4,923). 14.IV.82

Fig 5
RICHARD WAGNER
An autograph letter to Franz Brendel, about *Tannhäuser*,
Lohengrin, Beethoven and Liszt, Zurich, 4 February 1852
London £1,320 ($2,363). 14.IV.82

Mozart and Beethoven and, in another letter, he writes about Mozart's Symphony
no 39 in E flat major, K 543 (Fig 4): he suggests various ways of performing the
opening of the slow movement and again gives a musical quotation to underline his
point. On other occasions, Wagner writes on more general matters of musical
aesthetics. There are two exceptionally interesting letters, apparently unpublished,
to Franz Brendel, editor of the *Neue Zeitung für Musik*, about the art of composition,
musical form and contemporary operatic music (*cf* Fig 5). These date from 1852–53,
some two years after Wagner's major theoretical work *Oper und Drama*.

Apart from letters, this group of manuscripts contains other items of great interest.
These include an unrecorded autograph draft of a short newspaper article, written for
the Munich *Neueste Nachrichten* in 1865. At this time, Wagner was under virulent
attack in the Munich press about his influence over Ludwig II, his financial affairs

Fig 6
RICHARD WAGNER
An autograph manuscript of the
Wahlspruch für die Deutsche Feuerwehr,
Luzern, 8 November 1869
London £3,960 ($7,088). 14.IV.82

and his mode of life. The article constitutes a stout defence of the composer and his work and was apparently meant to be published under von Bülow's name. Wagner seems to have been especially fond of this kind of 'anonymity'; his notorious *Das Judenthum in der Musik* was ascribed to one 'K. Freigedank', though in a letter to Ferdinand Heine (14 September 1850), Wagner freely admits his authorship.

Finally, there are two examples of Wagner's music. The first is a memento of the Paris production of *Rienzi* in 1869. It consists of the prayer melody from the opera with Wagner's signature below. The other manuscript dates from later that same year (Fig 6). Cosima Wagner's diary for 9 November tells us: 'Richard is asked for a tribute to the firemen, which he immediately drafts.'[1] Cosima's memory seems to be at fault, for Wagner's manuscript of his *Wahlspruch für die Deutsche Feuerwehr* is actually dated 'Lużern 8 Nov. 1869'. The piece is a slight one, comprising nine bars for four-part male voice choir, but such a manuscript is a rarity in the saleroom. The music has an authentic Wagnerian flavour, particularly the surprise modulation in the third phrase, which stirs memories of Siegfried's motif in *The Ring*.

The riches of this group of letters and manuscripts are manifold, offering insights into all facets of Wagner's life. Throughout them all, however, runs the thread of Wagner's work and their fascination lies in the way they chronicle the development of his creations, together with his ideas about them. Since the dispersal of the Burrell Collection and the publication of so much documentary material about Wagner during the 1970s, new source material has become increasingly rare. The amount of unpublished material, therefore, in this group makes its appearance in the saleroom a major event, and an appropriate herald of the centenary of Wagner's death, in 1983.

[1] *Cosima Wagner's Diaries* ed Gregor-Dellin and Mack, trans Skelton, Vol 1 (London, 1978) p 163

Coins and medals

The Tibet medal group awarded to Colonel Sir Francis
Younghusband, commander of the first expedition to Tibet in 1903
London £3,600 ($6,444). 4.III.82
From the collection of the late Dame Eileen Younghusband

The Victoria Cross medal group for 'D-Day' awarded to CSM Stanley Hollis, The Green Howards
London £32,000 ($57,280). 4.III.82
This was the only Victoria Cross awarded for 'D-Day'

VIKING DANELAW,
imitation penny of Alfred
the Great (871–99 AD)
London £1,600 ($2,864).
21.I.82

ENGLAND, gold half-noble of Henry VI
(1422–61), annulet and leaf-trefoil issues
London £11,000 ($19,690). 12.XI.81
No other half-noble of the leaf-trefoil
issue is known

ANGLO-SAXON, second
jewel cross penny of
Harthacnut (first reign
1035–37), Exeter mint
London £1,450 ($2,596).
12.XI.81

OTTOMAN, gold sultani of
Mohammed II, AH 882
(1477 AD), Constantinople
mint
London £3,000 ($5,370).
28.IV.82

SASANIAN,
gold stater of
Varhran VI
(590–91 AD)
London £4,200
($7,518).
20.V.82

AUSTRALIA, gold pound, 1852,
Adelaide Assay Office
London £4,800 ($8,592). 12.XI.81

UNITED STATES OF
AMERICA, half-dollar,
1796
New York $19,800
(£11,061). 14.I.82

GERMANY, Lower Bavaria, silver medal
of Sebastian, Count of Ortenburg,
circa 1530
London £1,800 ($3,222). 18.III.82

ENGLAND, Lancaster
halfpenny token, 1794
New York $1,980
(£1,106). 8.XII.81
From the collection of
John R. Farnell Sr

ROMAN, aureus of Domitian, with Germania mourning on the reverse, *circa* 88 AD
SFr 39,600
(£11,061:$19,799)

Left
ROMAN, aureus of Mark Antony, struck to pay the Sixth Legion, *circa* 32 BC
SFr 60,500
(£16,899:$30,249)

Right
ROMAN, aureus of Macrinus (217–18 AD), with Securitas on the reverse
SFr 77,000
(£21,508:$38,499)

ROMAN, 5 aurei medallion of Galerius Maximian as Caesar, with Mars in victory on the reverse, 297 AD, Trier mint
SFr 275,000 (£76,816:$137,501)

The above medallion is one of only two known extant examples, both from the hoard found near Arras, France, in 1922. It commemorates the reconquest of Britain in 296 AD, when the forces of Constantius Chlorus defeated the usurper Allectus in Hampshire. The hoard itself was one of the greatest numismatic discoveries this century but its importance was diminished by the melting of a substantial portion which were wrongly condemned as forgeries

ROMAN, aureus of Caracalla, with his parents Septimius Severus and Julia Domna on the reverse, 201 AD
SFr 39,600
(£11,061:$19,799)

Left
ROMAN, aureus of Julia Domna, with her sons Caracalla and Geta on the reverse, 201 AD
SFr 47,300
(£13,212:$23,649)

Right
ROMAN, aureus of Postumus, with the seated emperor on the reverse, 263 AD
SFr 46,200
(£12,905:$23,100)

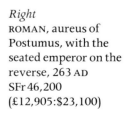

The gold coins illustrated on this page are from the Virgil M. Brand Collection and were sold in Zurich on 1 July 1982

Left
POLAND, 10 ducats of Vladislaus IV
by Johann Höhn, 1635
SFr 49,500 (£13,827:$24,750)

Right
ITALY, Retegno, 10 zecchini of
Theodore Trivulzio, 1677
SFr 66,000 (£18,436:$33,000)

GERMANY, Anhalt-Zerbst, commemorative gulden struck in gold
of Johann Ludwig and Christian August, 1745
SFr 24,200 (£6,760:$12,100)

ITALY, Naples,
40 franchi of
Gioacchino Murat,
1810
SFr 82,500
(£23,045:$41,251)

ITALY, Naples, ducat of
Frederick III of Aragon
(1496–1501)
SFr 19,250
(£5,377:$9,625)

RIGA, 5 ducats of Karl X Gustavus of Sweden
by Sebastian Dadler, 1654
SFr 22,000 (£6,145:$11,000)

The gold coins illustrated on this page are from the Virgil M. Brand Collection and were sold in Zurich on 1 July 1982

Arms and armour

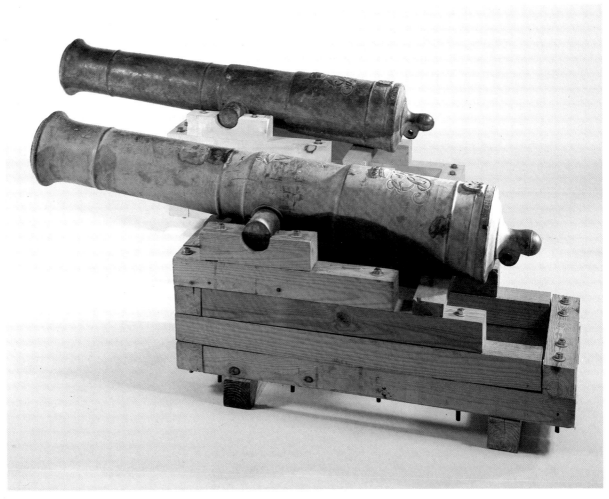

A pair of George II twelve-pound cannon by Andrew Schalch, each signed and dated *1748*, length of each 65½in (166.5cm)
New York $74,800 (£41,788). 22.V.82

This price represents the highest bid at auction, inclusive of premium: ownership is the subject of a legal dispute

Andrew Schalch was born in Switzerland in 1692 and trained as a cannon founder in France. After coming to England, he was appointed Master Founder of the newly built Royal Brass Foundry at Woolwich, in 1716, and worked there as master until 1770. These cannon were found in Lake Champlain, New York, in September 1968 and were probably used by British forces at Fort George, until its capture by the French in 1757. They may then have been removed to Fort Ticonderoga and lost from one of the French galleys sunk in October 1759

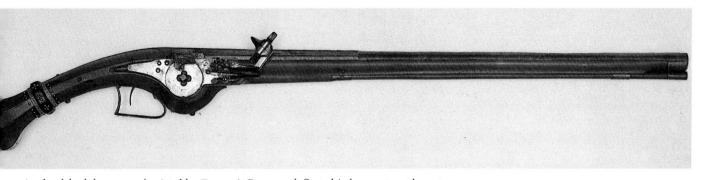

A wheel-lock horseman's pistol by François Poumerol, first third seventeenth century, length 26⅜in (67cm)
London £28,600($51,194). 20.IV.82

François Poumerol was *arquebusier* to Gaston, Duke of Orléans, brother of Louis XIII

One of a pair of db 12-bore side-lock self-opening ejector sporting guns by J. Purdey & Sons, serial numbers 28003/28004, 1975, length 45½in (115.6cm)
Gleneagles £19,800($35,442). 31.VIII.81

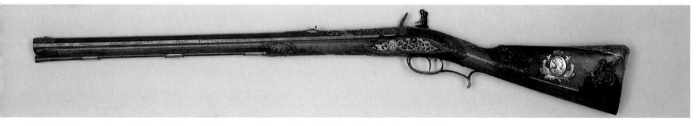

A flintlock sporting rifle by Johann Sebastian Hauschka, Wolfenbüttel, dated *1733*, length 41½in (105.4cm)
London £11,550($20,675). 20.IV.82

Johann Sebastian Hauschka was appointed court gunmaker to the Duke of Braunschweig-Wolfenbüttel in 1721

Works of art

A Nottingham alabaster altarpiece, second half fifteenth century, width 65in (165.1cm)
London £49,500 ($88,605). 24.VI.82
Acquired for the Castle Museum, Nottingham, with the aid of a grant from the National Art-Collections Fund

Four panels show scenes from the Passion – the Betrayal, the Flagellation, the Entombment and the Resurrection – with a central panel depicting the Trinity. The only other complete altarpiece known in England in its original frame is the Swansea altarpiece in the Victoria and Albert Museum, London

A Flemish ivory group of the Virgin and Child with St John the Baptist, attributed to the school of
François Duquesnoy, *circa* 1650, height of group 12½in (31.7cm)
London £15,400 ($27,566). 10.XII.81

A bronze figure of an angel, possibly English, mid fifteenth century, height 34in (86.4cm)
New York $121,000 (£67,598). 27.XI.81

This figure was formerly in Horace Walpole's house and is shown in the frontispiece to the *Description of the Villa of Mr Horace Walpole at Strawberry Hill, near Twickenham* (1784), in which it is described as follows: 'Entering by the great North Gate, the first object that presents itself is a small oratory enclosed with iron rails; in front, an altar, on which stands a saint in bronze'

An Italian ivory figure probably of Cosimo de' Medici (1519–74), sixteenth century, height 11¾in (29.8cm)
New York $154,000(£86,034). 27.XI.81

This ivory was previously in the Mentmore Collection, selling for £33,000 on 23 May 1977

A bronze figure of Minerva by Johann Gregor van der Schardt, *circa* 1570–75, height 20$\frac{7}{8}$in (53cm)
London £99,000($177,210). 24.VI.82

Johann Gregor van der Schardt was born in Nijmegen, *circa* 1530, and worked in Rome, Bologna and
Venice. This bronze was acquired by the collector Paul von Praun in Bologna, at the end of the
sixteenth century and it remained in the collection of his descendants, in Nuremberg, until 1801

'The Fair Maid of Gatacre'

John Hayward

Renaissance jewellery is almost always anonymous, with original source, designer, maker and owner all unknown. The appearance at auction of a jewel, which could be identified as English and which had remained in the possession of a Shropshire family ever since the sixteenth century, was therefore a rare occasion (Fig 1).

The Gatacre family can be traced back in Shropshire to the time of Edward the Confessor and a William de Gatacre is mentioned in a Pipe Roll of 1160. The jewel was known in the family as 'The Fair Maid of Gatacre'; according to family tradition it was so named after its first wearer, Mary, who was renowned for her beauty. The eldest daughter of Robert Gatacre (1495–after 1559) of Gatacre Hall, Shropshire, she married John Wolryche of Dudmaston, near Bridgnorth, in 1528. The jewel is said to have been worn in subsequent generations by the eldest daughters of the family in succession until the time of their marriage. Like most family traditions, the story of The Fair Maid of Gatacre cannot be accepted at face value, as the Mannerist design of the jewel precludes a date before the last quarter of the sixteenth century. If it were first worn by the Mary Gatacre who married John Wolryche, then it must have received a new setting later in the century. Its remarkable state of preservation suggests that the Gatacre daughters were allowed to wear it only on rare occasions.

The enamelled gold frame with three pendent pearls (missing at the time of the auction but since restored) can be attributed to a London goldsmith. This attribution is confirmed by its close similarity to a drawing (Fig 2) in the book of jewels in the Victoria and Albert Museum, which is believed to have belonged to Arnold Lulls, a Flemish-born merchant who supplied jewellery to the court of James I and Anne of Denmark. He was one of the many Flemish Protestants who emigrated from Antwerp, then the chief European centre of the jeweller's art, to escape the Spanish Inquisition introduced by the Duke of Alva. The frames of both the Gatacre jewel and the Lulls drawing are composed of conventionalized interlacing snakes, with bodies enamelled white. In place of the cameo in the centre of the former, the Lulls jewel is centred on a large table-cut emerald framed by diamonds and a ring of pavé-set rubies. The most important part of the Gatacre jewel is not the setting but the Roman, probably third-century AD, amethyst cameo it encloses. It resembles, though on a smaller scale, the magnificent Roman Medusa-head cameo, also carved in amethyst, in the British Museum, which is possibly somewhat earlier in date. No snakes are visible in the hair of the Gatacre cameo, which must, therefore, represent the mask of Perseus. Both

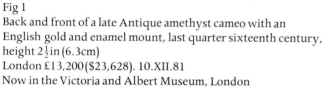

Fig 1
Back and front of a late Antique amethyst cameo with an
English gold and enamel mount, last quarter sixteenth century,
height 2½in (6.3cm)
London £13,200 ($23,628). 10.XII.81
Now in the Victoria and Albert Museum, London

Fig 2
A watercolour drawing of an early
seventeenth-century English
pendant from the workshop of
Arnold Lulls
Reproduced courtesy of the
Victoria and Albert Museum,
London

Medusa and Perseus masks were popular subjects in the Roman empire, one of the largest extant being the British Museum amethyst.

The classical Roman source of the cameo raises another problem – how did a Shropshire country gentleman acquire so rare and ancient an object? The most likely member of the family to have obtained such a treasure was William Gatacre (1506–77), son and heir of Robert Gatacre and elder brother of Mary, after whom the jewel is said to have been named. William Gatacre was Escheator of the County of Shropshire between 1524 and 1542, an office which carried the duty of seizing properties confiscated by the Crown. This could have involved dealing with secularized monasteries and their treasures. Medieval shrines, crosses and cult objects were sometimes profusely adorned with classical cameos because they were mistakenly thought to have early Christian associations. An adherent of the Roman Catholic Church, William Gatacre may have rescued the cameo of the Gatacre jewel from destruction when the liturgical object to which it was attached was sent to the melting pot, had it mounted in London, and established it as a family heirloom.

A South German gilt-bronze relief of the Virgin
and Child with St Anne, late sixteenth century,
height of relief 12⅝in (32cm)
London £11,000 ($19,690). 10.XII.81

The Italian wood frame is of a later date

A pearwood holy-water stoup,
Flemish or Dutch, *circa* 1690, height 20in (50.8cm)
London £5,500 ($9,845). 22.IV.82

A terracotta figure of a girl bearing
offerings by Joseph-Charles Marin,
signed and dated *1793*,
height 23in (58.5cm)
Monte Carlo FF 99,900
(£9,115:$16,316). 14.VI.82

A bronze and enamel group of St George and the dragon by Sir Alfred Gilbert, *circa* 1890, height of group 9½in (24.1cm)
London £5,720($10,239). 16.VI.82

This bronze is probably a maquette for the top of a rose-water dish and ewer designed for the officers of the Brigade of Guards and presented to the Duke of York, later George V, on the occasion of his marriage in 1893

A bronze figure of a young woman by Hippolyte Moreau, signed, Paris, *circa* 1890, height 43¾in (111cm)
London £3,410($6,104). 18.VI.82

A pair of marble figures, *Morning* by Edgar George Papworth, signed and dated *1863*, and *Night* by Edward William Wyon, signed and dated *1868*, height of each figure 50in (127cm); 41in (104cm)
London £9,350 ($16,737). 18.VI.82

Cretan icons

Manolis Chatzidakis

Icons hold an increasing fascination, both as objects of religious veneration and as works of art. Their particular nature is determined by a number of factors. On the one hand, through the Byzantine and post-Byzantine era, the art of the icon is governed by an unchanging structure of ideas. Orthodox theology has consistently maintained that the icon is an intermediary between the physical world of the senses and the divine world. It provides a terrestrial representation of a heavenly archetype. This capacity to represent the heavenly archetype enables the icon to be a medium for Divine Grace. When Grace manifests itself, through miracle working, the icon becomes a prototype in its own right, so that Divine Grace cannot then be transmitted to another icon unless it follows the same iconography and reflects it faithfully. This explains the conservatism of the art of the icon, and the persistence of themes – both in the composition of scenes from religious history and the stylized portraiture of biblical figures and saints.

On the other hand, the painting of icons, panel paintings, sprang from the great tradition of late classical art, which furnished a technique, a style and models for themes and motifs, lasting throughout the Middle Ages. Thus, the best icons, themselves magnificent works of art, contain a delayed echo of the classical tradition of Hellenistic art. The finest Byzantine icons were painted in Constantinople, guardian of classical tradition, in either the court workshops or those of a number of famous monasteries, by artists whose talent was matched only by their fervent piety. In time, the practice of this ancient art form led to refinements in the art of painting which themselves became part of the artistic tradition.

After the fall of Constantinople in 1453, the cultural and religious life of Byzantium survived and continued to evolve, in spite of the disappearance of the great centres of artistic and cultural production, Constantinople and Thessalonica. The artists of the Byzantine diaspora sought new places in which to continue the production of icons, to satisfy a growing demand. It was the towns of the island of Crete, under Venetian control since 1204, which were to assume the task of continuing the classical tradition. Indeed, a number of painters from Constantinople had taken refuge there from the beginning of the fifteenth century. These artists were to bring the best traditions of the art of the empire to the provincial Byzantine art of the island. Under somewhat indulgent Venetian rule, the 'Cretan school' flourished. It was the most important school in the contemporary Orthodox world and was to last until the end of the Venetian occupation in 1669.

Fig 1
A Cretan icon of the Mother of God 'Hodegetria', second half fifteenth century,
33⅛in by 25¾in (84cm by 65.5cm)
London £20,900. 15.VI.81

A large number of artists worked continuously in the production of icons, mainly of the Virgin, above all at Candia (Heraklion). A high proportion were exported to the West, where conservative Catholics remained attached to their spiritual value and the technical skill of the gilding and tempera. To some western Christians, Cretan icons were perhaps the only works of the post-Renaissance era to retain an 'odour of sanctity'. Major Orthodox monasteries, as well as the Greek and Catholic bourgeoisie, were also among the best patrons.

Fig 2
A Cretan icon of the Mother of God 'tou Pathou', first
half sixteenth century, 25⅝in by 20⅞in (65cm by 53cm)
London £18,150($32,489). 10.VI.82

Fig 3
An icon of the Mother of God 'Eleoussa', probably
the Greek Islands, first half sixteenth century,
18¼in by 13½in (46.5cm by 34.2cm)
London £6,050($10,830). 7.XII.81

It is in a series of icons of the Virgin that one can best assess the capacity of this art
for variety of expression, within a framework of repeated iconographic types and
conventions for modelling and drapery. Figure 1 repeats an age-old type of Virgin,
the 'Hodegetria'. The precision of drawing, the elegance of form, and the sensitivity
in treatment of face and hands, place this work among the best Cretan icons of the
second half of the fifteenth century. In the minute gold delineation of the clothing,
reminiscent of engraving, the tooled halo and the perfect gilt background this
masterpiece attains to the splendour of goldsmiths' work.

In a second icon (see *Art at Auction 1980–81*, p 350), it is possible to recognize the
same qualities of technical perfection, but the artist has returned to fourteenth-century
models accentuating a sense of volume. There is also a certain deliberate ugliness in
the face of the child Jesus, of anti-classical origin. This icon, dating from *circa* 1500, is
of another ancient Byzantine type, the 'Eleoussa', or Virgin of Tenderness. It is
interesting to note that in both these icons, created using the same techniques and
within the same style, there is a supplementary figurative element: two little
archangels accompany the Virgin and almost constitute a stamp of origin. A Virgin of
the Passion, or 'tou Pathou', also contains the archangels, but is probably of a slightly
later date (Fig 2). The child turns towards the approaching symbols of the Passion.

Fig 4
A Cretan triptych, the obverse of the left-hand panel showing St Peter and St Paul, and the reverse
showing St George, *circa* 1500, the triptych 9in by 17⅛in (23cm by 43.5cm)
London £5,500. 15.VI.81

A second Virgin of Tenderness is of a different type (Fig 3). Probably produced
sometime during the first half of the sixteenth century, this Virgin must derive from a
Cretan archetype which had been strongly influenced by earlier Italian art. This is
clear from the naked upper half of the child's body and arms. A lack of finesse in the
drawing, rather too abstract facial expressions and a clumsiness in the preparation of
the wood panel suggest that it is a copy, perhaps from the Greek Islands.

The ability of several Cretan icon painters to work in two quite different styles
should not be surprising. These artists lived in towns of Italianate appearance, where
Italian, and even Flemish painters were well established and where Italian works of
art were to be found in Catholic churches and the mansions of the wealthy bourgeoisie.
Thus, side by side with traditional Greek icons, painters provided their western
clientèle with '*ancone*', taking their inspiration from Tuscan or, more often, Venetian
paintings. Frequently, they worked in both styles on the same piece, with figures
belonging sometimes to the *maniera greca*, sometimes to the *maniera italiana*. This is
the case for a triptych sold recently. Like other pieces in the same genre, designed for
private worship, the central section contains a 'Madre di Consolazione' in the Italian
style, while the leaves are pure Cretan (Fig 4). There is no doubt that this piece was
executed by a single Cretan artist, *circa* 1500, for a Catholic customer.

Fig 5
A Cretan icon of St George, *circa* 1480–1500, 38⅝in by 32⅛in (98cm by 81.5cm)
London £36,300 ($64,977). 7. XII.81

Fig 6 *Opposite*
An icon of Joseph's dream by Theodor Poulakis, second half seventeenth century, 18⅛in by 21in
(46cm by 53.5cm)
London £16,500 ($29,535). 10.VI.82

A fine icon of St George on horseback slaying the dragon (Fig 5) illustrates the integration of elements derived from the two distinct styles. The dragon owes much to western iconography and it has been suggested that the rearing horse bears the influence of fifteenth-century Italian works, such as the *St George* by Paolo Veneziano. It is a version of what appears to have been a famous prototype, the nearest example to this lost piece being in the Museum of the Hellenic Institute, Venice. The archetype was to become an established part of fifteenth-century and later Cretan art.

Cretan painting continued to flourish and evolve until the end of the seventeenth century. An important icon of the Tree of Jesse, signed by the painter Theodor Poulakis (d 1692), a native of Canea, is a very fine example of the varied work of this artist, who spent his life in Corfu and Venice (see *Art at Auction 1980–81*, p351). This piece is in his most traditional, thus his most coherent, style. In a series of icons illustrating the stories of the Old Testament, based on Flemish engravings, the spirit is much more baroque, despite the Byzantine legacy (Fig 6).

A Fabergé silver-gilt and nephrite desk set, comprising a desk lamp, letter rack, pen tray and paperweight, workmaster Julius Rappoport; an inkstand, vase, abacus and blotter, workmaster Victor Aarne; a vesta case, workmaster Hjalmar Armfelt; and a desk seal, ashtray, stamp dampener and waste-paper basket, unmarked; St Petersburg, 1899–1908, height of lamp 26³⁄₈in (67cm)
Geneva SFr 264,000 (£73,743:$132,000). 7.V.82

Above, from left to right
A silver-gilt and enamel Easter egg, maker's mark of N. V.
Alekseyev, Moscow, *circa* 1900. $5,500 (£3,073)
A Fabergé jewelled, silver-gilt and shaded enamel Easter
egg, workmaster Fedor Rückert, Moscow, *circa* 1910.
$14,300 (£7,989)
A silver-gilt and shaded enamel Easter egg, Moscow,
circa 1900. $4,620 (£2,581)
A silver-gilt and enamel Easter egg, maker's mark of
N. W. Nemirov-Kolodkin, Moscow, *circa* 1900.
$3,520 (£1,966)
From the collection of the National Cathedral,
Washington DC
A Fabergé silver-gilt and shaded enamel Easter egg,
workmaster Fedor Rückert, Moscow, *circa* 1900.
$15,400 (£8,603)

Below, from left to right
A silver-gilt and *champlevé* enamel Easter egg, late
nineteenth century. $1,870 (£1,045)
A silver-gilt and enamel Easter egg, maker's mark *G. P.,*
circa 1900. $3,300 (£1,844)
A silver-gilt and shaded enamel Easter egg, maker's mark
of Ivan Khlebnikov, Moscow, *circa* 1900. $7,975 (£4,455)
A Fabergé silver-gilt and shaded enamel Easter egg,
workmaster Fedor Rückert, Moscow, *circa* 1900.
$16,500 (£9,218)
From the collection of the National Cathedral,
Washington DC

The Easter eggs illustrated on this page were sold in New York on 14 December 1981

A silver-gilt and niello coffee pot, maker's mark probably *S.I.*, and mark of alderman Fedor Petrov, Moscow, 1777, height 9⅛in (23.2cm)
London £5,060 ($9,057). 21.VI.82

Below
A set of six Fabergé gold and enamel vodka *charki*, workmaster Mikhail Perchin, St Petersburg, late nineteenth century, height 1¾in (4.3cm)
London £19,800 ($35,442). 21.VI.82

A gold and enamel snuff box, maker's mark of Jean Ducrollay, Paris, 1742, width 3⅛in (8cm)
London £57,200 ($102,388). 21.VI.82

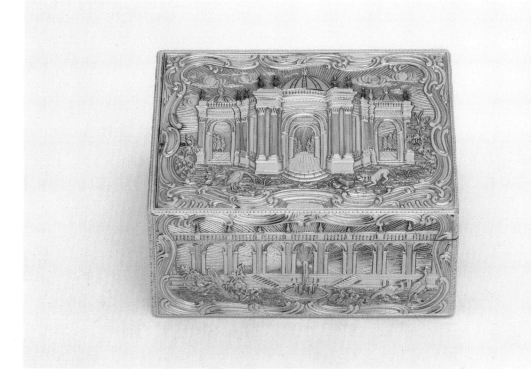

A four-colour gold snuff box, maker's mark of Louis-Guillaume Cassé, Paris, 1755–56,
width 3⅜in (8.5cm)
London £45,100 ($80,729). 21.VI.82

A gold snuff box, maker's mark *F.H.*, possibly for
Francis Harrache, London, 1741, width 2⅞in (7.2cm)
London £16,500 ($29,535). 7.XII.81

A gold and hardstone snuff box by Johann Christian
Neuber, Dresden, *circa* 1770, width 2¾in (6.9cm)
London £24,200 ($43,318). 21.VI.82

A Swiss four-colour gold and enamel snuff box, *circa*
1830, width 4in (10.2cm)
New York $23,100 (£12,905). 15.IV.82

A jewelled, gold and enamel presentation snuff box,
marked *I. F. Reiss B.*, German or Swiss, *circa* 1860,
width 3⅜in (8.5cm)
New York $33,000 (£18,436). 15.IV.82

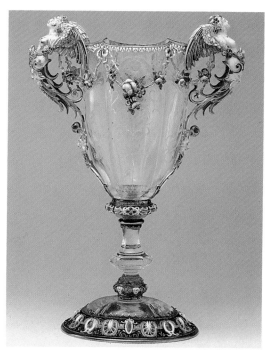

A Swiss jewelled three-colour gold and enamel scent bottle, maker's mark *F.F.*, *circa* 1780, height 4⅜in (11cm)
Geneva SFr 24,200(£6,760:$12,100). 11.XI.81

A rock-crystal cup with gold and enamel mounts by Jean-Valentin Morel, *circa* 1850, height 8½in (21.5cm)
London £14,300($25,597). 21.VI.82

An enamel *boîte à surprise*, probably London, *circa* 1765, width 3⅜in (8.5cm)
London £5,060($9,057). 2.II.82

ISAAC OLIVER
A nobleman, on vellum,
signed and dated *1617*,
$2\frac{1}{8}$in (5.3cm)
London £8,250($14,768).
19.X.81

STUDIO OF PETER OLIVER
A nobleman, called Robert
Dormer, Earl of Carnarvon, on
vellum, *circa* 1635, $2\frac{1}{8}$in (5.3cm)
London £4,840($8,664). 19.X.81

PETER CROSS
Robert Kerr, 4th Earl of Lothian, on vellum,
signed and dated *1667*, 3in (7.6cm)
London £9,020($16,146). 19.X.81
Now in the Victoria and Albert Museum,
London

THOMAS FLATMAN
Sir Geoffrey Palmer, Bt, Attorney General, on
vellum, signed and dated *1663*, $2\frac{5}{8}$in (6.6cm)
London £6,380($11,420). 19.X.81

RICHARD COSWAY
The Hon Henry Frederick and the Lady Anne
Compton Cavendish, signed and dated *1792* on the
reverse, $3\frac{1}{4}$in (8.2cm)
London £10,120($18,115). 19.X.81
From the collection of the Rt Hon the Earl Cawdor

JOHN SMART
Lady Fanny Chambers, signed and
dated *1792 I*, $2\frac{1}{2}$in (6.5cm)
London £7,920($14,177). 13.VII.82

JOHN SMART
Muhammad Ali Khan, Nawab of Arcot
and Prince of the Carnatic, signed and
dated *1791 I*, $2\frac{7}{8}$in (7.3cm)
London £5,720($10,239). 19.X.81

RICHARD COSWAY
Anne, Countess of Mountnorris,
circa 1790, 3in (7.6cm)
London £9,240($16,540). 19.X.81

A pair of portrait miniatures by Jean-Honoré Fragonard

Eunice Williams

Last year, a pair of previously unknown, unpublished miniatures appeared in the hands of a collector and captured the attention of all who saw them (see opposite). Protected under panels of glass and framed in gold, these excellently preserved watercolours formed the covers of an *aide-mémoire*. Although they were unsigned, the name of Jean-Honoré Fragonard (1732–1806) came immediately to mind because, as the Goncourts wrote: 'Fragonard's drawing is his handwriting.'

The subject of each miniature is a child in fancy costume; it is unlikely that they are specific likenesses. One young boy is dressed in a floppy Pierrot tunic, the second as a fencer with a ruffled collar and sword. In the eighteenth century this costume was called 'Spanish', although it owed more to Rubens and the *Commedia dell'arte* than to Spain. The theatrical connotations are subtle, but they reinforce the idealization of the children. Such rôle playing is not without interest in a period of social change: François-Hubert Drouais, a colleague of Fragonard's, depicted royal and aristocratic children in the humble guises of savoyard musicians and montagnards; and Marie Antoinette dressed as a shepherdess to play in her *hameau*.

Certainly among the most important miniatures to come on the market recently, this pair has an obscure history. The *aide-mémoire* is probably a little later in date than the miniatures. Inscriptions on the book's pages provide the only clues to its provenance. A dedication to an unnamed lady is signed *Pierre D de Courlande*. Two Dukes of Kurland, a Baltic duchy then under Polish protection, bore the name Pierre de Biren; the elder died in 1772, his son in 1800. The stylistic dating of the *aide-mémoire* could fall within the lifespan of the latter. From the continent, the luxurious little volume apparently found its way to England. On later pages are inscribed the names *Fortescue/1817, Hannibal/Macclesfield, Fortescue Hugh, Margaret, Ld Robt Carr* and *The Empress Elizabeth*.

None of these names appears in the list of collectors who owned or sold miniatures attributed to Fragonard, published in Roger Portalis's monograph on the artist (1889). Portalis included four representations of Pierrot, mostly of oval shape, but only one described as a fencer; two oval miniatures, not necessarily a pair, one *Jeune garçon costumé en Pierrot* and one *Enfant à l'épée*, were in the Muhlbacher Collection. A rectangular version of the latter, unknown to Portalis, was shown in 1912 at the Brussels exhibition of miniatures. The lender was M. Kapferer of Paris. By 1921, it

JEAN-HONORE FRAGONARD
A pair of miniatures, Pierrot and a fencer, mounted in gold as the covers of an *aide-mémoire, circa* 1770, each 3¼in (8.2cm)
Geneva SFr110,000 (£30,726:$55,000). 7.V.82

was in the David-Weill Collection, when it was lent to the Fragonard exhibition at the Pavillon de Marsan. Almost identical to *The fencer* sold at Sotheby's, it is now in the Louvre (Donation de David-Weill, 543).

Fragonard was a versatile and prolific artist. In addition to the paintings and drawings, a group of approximately two dozen miniatures has been traditionally linked to his name. While they bear a superficial resemblance to his other works, they are not homogeneous in quality or style, and it has been questioned whether Fragonard ever painted miniatures at all. In the absence of signed examples, some writers dismiss the group on the grounds that the master would have been too occupied with regular commissions to involve himself in such a specialized field. Perhaps enhancing this view is the fact that Fragonard's wife, Marie-Anne Gérard, was a miniature painter before and during their marriage, and exhibited professionally. The easy answer has been to have the couple share attributions, but such a conclusion is obviously unsatisfactory. This is a topic deserving further study; it is necessary to examine the works within the context of Fragonard's total *oeuvre*.

This pair of miniatures reflect themes and techniques associated with the artist. The lively surface and freely applied colour correspond to Fragonard's characteristic style of working, whatever the media. A miniaturist only by avocation, he treats the small pictures as if they were larger portraits. The quality and boldness of handling and the sophisticated pictorial conception are impressive. Vigorous, succinct and seemingly effortless brush strokes only partially cover the broadly sketched, angular under-drawing, which remains visible just as it does in Fragonard's wash drawings. Both *Pierrot* and *The fencer* pose before blank backgrounds. Lighting is controlled to suggest space behind and around the models. The ivory ground is lightly covered with unblended strokes of mottled colour graduated through several values. Fragonard regularly employed such a *tacheté* background for portraits, as did David after him. In the nineteenth century, it became a common feature of portrait miniatures.

There are pertinent parallels between these miniatures and well-known, authentic easel pictures by Fragonard. When *Pierrot* is compared to the oil painting of a *Boy dressed as Pierrot* (Wallace Collection, London), it is evident that the miniature is not merely a copy of the larger work, as has been suggested by some commentators. Not only are the two sitters of different ages and colouring, but their poses separate them as well. The Wallace Collection *Boy* stands upright and frontal, while the younger child in the miniature leans forward on the diagonal.

The fencer invites comparison with Fragonard's portraits of men and women garbed *à l'espagnole*, such as the dramatic series of *Figures de fantaisie*, dated *circa* 1769. In spite of the contrasting moods and ages of the subjects, there are similar colour harmonies and, most striking, formal analogies that demonstrate Fragonard's skill at foreshortening an arm and summarily indicating a fist with swash-buckling ease. The artist's personality pervades his brushwork.

Chronology is a problem throughout Fragonard's *oeuvre*; it is almost impossible to date the miniatures precisely. There is no reason to assume that all were painted at the same time or even in the same decade. Fragonard did not work in such an organized manner. For now, it is important to recognize those miniatures which are autograph, such as *Pierrot* and *The fencer*. Because the pair share stylistic similarities with the *Figures de fantaisie*, a date *circa* 1770 might be proposed.

This period would be appropriate because it coincides with the beginning of Fragonard's long friendship with the Swedish artist, Pierre Adolphe Hall. Gifted as both painter and miniaturist, Hall brought new life to miniature painting, in that he employed broad strokes of freely blended colours rather than the meticulous *pointilliste* style that had been dominant. His lively brushwork may have been inspired by Fragonard's style of painting, for, besides their friendship, Hall owned several works by the artist. Conversely, Fragonard's interest in miniatures may have been provoked and encouraged by Hall. Much remains to be written about their influence on each other. For now, chronology of Fragonard's miniatures remains a puzzle, dependent upon interpretations of circumstantial evidence as much as stylistic criteria.

VAN BLARENBERGHE
Figures in a pleasure garden, on vellum, signed, *circa*
1780, 3⅛in (8cm)
Geneva SFr 30,800(£8,603:$15,399). 11.XI.81

JEAN-BAPTISTE AUGUSTIN
Madame de Sartigues with her daughter,
signed and dated *1793*, 3⅛in (8cm)
Geneva SFr 11,550(£3,226:$5,775). 7.V.82

ALOIS VON ANREITER after MORITZ MICHAEL
DAFFINGER
Maria Geroldstein, signed, *circa* 1830, 3⅛in (8cm)
Geneva SFr 9,350(£2,612:$4,675). 7.V.82
From the collection of HSH the Prince of
Liechtenstein

PIETER VAN SLINGELAND
A gentleman, on panel, signed, *circa* 1675, 4⅛in
(10.5cm)
Geneva SFr 9,900(£2,765:$4,949). 11.XI.81

Clocks and watches

BREGUET NO 2489
A gold cased minute-repeating clockwatch, Paris,
diameter $2\frac{1}{8}$in (5.3cm)
Geneva SFr 96,800 (£27,039:$48,400). 10.XI.81

CHARLES CABRIER NO 7682
A gold and agate cased verge
timepiece, London, mid eighteenth
century, height $2\frac{1}{2}$in (6.5cm)
London £24,200 ($43,318). 18.II.82

TAVERNIER NO 439
A gold cased double-dialled dumb quarter-
repeating calendar verge watch, Paris, second
half eighteenth century, diameter $1\frac{7}{8}$in (4.8cm)
Geneva SFr 49,500 (£13,827:$24,750). 10.XI.81

A Swiss gold and enamel verge watch by Henry
Martin, late eighteenth century,
diameter $2\frac{3}{8}$in (6.1cm)
Geneva SFr 44,000 (£12,291:$22,001). 10.XI.81

A brass graphometer by Michael Scheffelt, Ulm, dated *1719*,
diameter 13¼in (33.8cm)
London £2,420($4,332). 15.VII.82

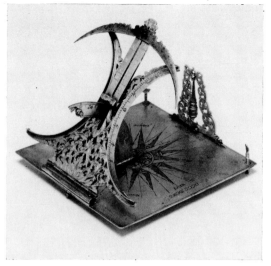

A silvered and gilt-metal equatorial sundial by
Johann Willebrand, Augsburg, *circa* 1710,
width 4⅝in (11.8cm)
London £11,550($20,675). 15.VII.82

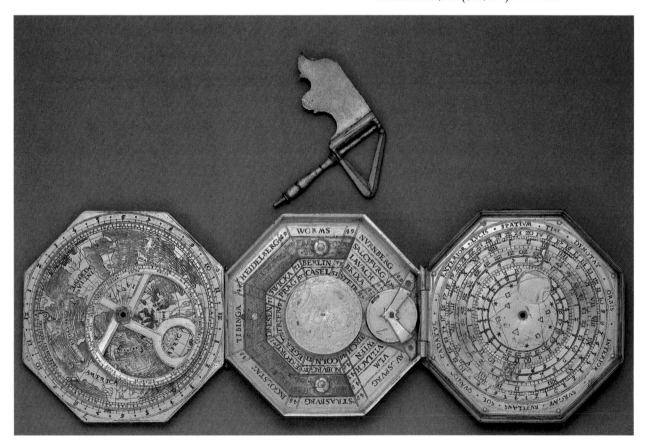

A gilt-metal compendium by Christopher Schissler, Augsburg, dated *1556*, width open 9in (22.8cm)
New York $35,200(£19,665). 14.VI.82

Nine English clocks

John Vaughan

The sale on 28 May 1982 of a collection of nine English clocks was a notable event in the annals of the clock department. Limited to the classic period of English clock-making between about 1670 and 1710, the collection was formed during and after the Second World War with the help of R. W. Symonds, author of the standard life of Thomas Tompion. Within this chosen field, the clocks formed a group of great interest and distinction, with each piece displaying different aspects of the clock-maker's and casemaker's art.

There were three Tompions: a turret clock of *circa* 1690, which was sold with an associated bell dated *1592*; an inlaid walnut quarter-repeating longcase clock; and a Tompion & Banger quarter-repeating bracket clock, dating from *circa* 1705, when Tompion was working in partnership with his nephew Edward Banger (Fig 5).

Three of the four clocks by Joseph Knibb deservedly realized the highest prices. The olivewood marquetry longcase, only 5 foot 6 inches high, is one of the very few early 'grandmother' clocks known (Fig 2). The dial is unusual in having the minutes numbered in full and a seconds ring. The veneering of the case is of the first quality. The silver-mounted ebony bracket clock has a rare form of *grande sonnerie* striking, typical of Knibb's unfailing inventiveness, and a dial of elegant yet restrained appearance (Fig 4). It had previously been sold at Sotheby's on 26 March 1954 for £1,200. The silver-mounted ebony alarum clock is in excellent original condition and is probably unique in retaining its turntable base (Fig 1). The architectural case and finely engraved backplate are other outstanding features of this noble clock.

The two remaining lots comprised a Christopher Gould longcase clock in a very good arabesque marquetry case, and a weight-driven ebony wall timepiece by Richard Street (Fig 3), with a delicately constructed fifteen-day movement. The hour ring is of irregular outline, the hour hand being fixed to the centre and guided by a cam so that its tip follows the inner edge. The dial plate is mounted with four silver cherubs and also engraved with a rose and thistle, probably to commemorate the Act of Union in 1707.

A large and expectant audience gathered for the sale; just over ten minutes later all was over. During this time, eight of the nine clocks were sold for a total of £361,350 ($646,817), at an average of over £40,000 per lot. The success of the sale is evidence of the continuing demand among discerning collectors for clocks by the great English makers, and of the enthusiasm aroused when a single collection is offered for sale at one time.

Fig 1
A silver-mounted ebony alarum turntable clock by Joseph Knibb, London, *circa* 1670,
height 25½in (64.8cm)
London £99,000 ($177,210). 28.V.82

Fig 3
An ebony wall timepiece by Richard Street, London,
circa 1707, height 3ft 6in (106.7cm)
London £24,200($43,318). 28.V.82

Fig 2 *Left*
An olivewood marquetry longcase clock by Joseph Knibb,
London, *circa* 1675, height 5ft 6in (167.7cm)
London £55,000($98,450). 28.V.82

Fig 4
A silver-mounted ebony *grande sonnerie* bracket clock by Joseph Knibb, London, *circa* 1675,
height 12in (30.5cm)
London £82,500 ($147,675). 28.V.82

Fig 5

TOMPION & BANGER NO 424

An ebony quarter-repeating bracket clock, London, *circa* 1705, height 14½in (36.8cm)
London £28,600($51,194). 28.V.82

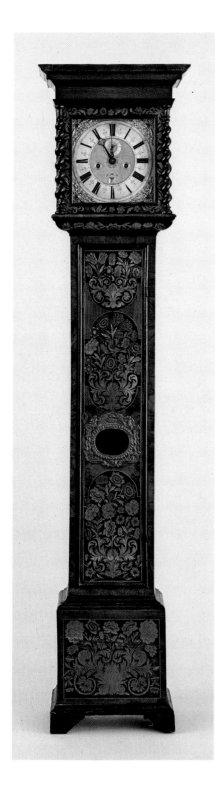

Left
A fruitwood marquetry month
longcase clock by David Le
Stourgeon, London, *circa* 1690,
height 7ft (213.5cm)
Los Angeles $16,500 (£9,218).
7.XII.81
From the collection of the late
William Rohkam Jr

Right
A Federal inlaid mahogany
longcase clock by Simon Willard,
Roxbury, Massachusetts,
circa 1790, height 8ft 1in
(246.5cm)
New York $77,000 (£43,017).
30.I.82
From the collection of the late
Joseph H. Hirshhorn

Musical instruments

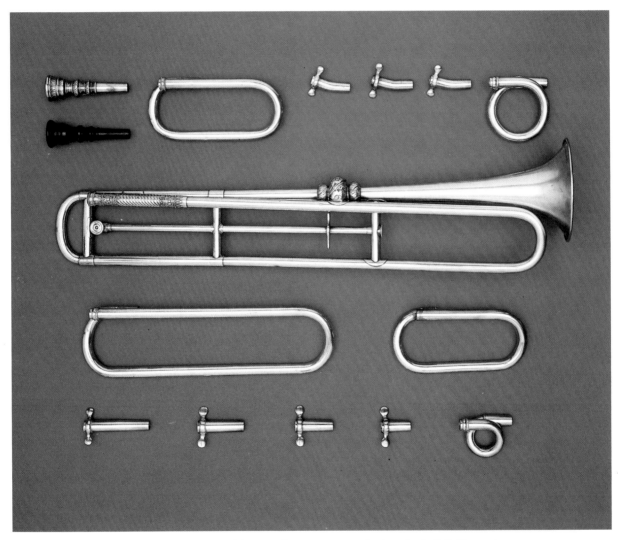

A silver slide trumpet by John Augustus Köhler, London, 1860, inscribed on the bell *T. Harper's Improved, Köhler, Maker, London*
London £2,530 ($4,529). 5.XI.81
From the collection of the Reverend J. A. Harper

This instrument belonged to Thomas J. Harper Junior (1816–98). He and his father, also Thomas Harper, were the leading English trumpeters of the nineteenth century, both holding the position of Sargeant Trumpeter to the Royal Household of Queen Victoria

A violin by Peter Guarneri of Venice, 1742, labelled *Petrus Guarnerius Filius Joseph Cremonensis fecit Venetiis. Anno 1742*, length of back $14\frac{1}{16}$ in (35.7cm) London £68,200 ($122,078). 7.IV.82

A violin by Jean-Baptiste Vuillaume, Paris, mid nineteenth century, labelled *Jean Baptiste Vuillaume a Paris, Rue Croix des Petits Champs*, length of back $14\frac{1}{8}$ in (35.9cm) London £17,600 ($31,504). 7.IV.82

Bressan and the Stanesbys

Maurice Byrne

Peter Bressan and the Thomas Stanesbys, father and son, were the leading woodwind-instrument makers in London in the early eighteenth century. Bressan was born in 1663 in Bourg-en-Bresse as Pierre Jaillard. His father died when he was young and he was apprenticed to a general wood turner in his home town for two years. He then probably went to Paris but had settled in London by 1690. Having an impossible French name, he called himself what he was, a Bressan; even this caused confusion to English scribes who wrote his name variously as Brisson, Brasson and even Brazoong. He joined a French Catholic community settled around Somerset House, which had briefly been Henrietta Maria's dower house. He lodged with one of her apothecaries, Claude Mignon, and in due course he married the apothecary's daughter.

On the death of his father-in-law, Bressan took over his rooms, which comprised part of Duchy House, on the east end of the decaying Palace of the Savoy. The house had been the London residence of the Chancellor of the Duchy of Lancaster, and the railings outside the present offices of the Duchy, by Waterloo Bridge, bear the same red rose of Lancaster with which Bressan marked all his instruments by way of giving his address. A similar maker's mark was adopted by Johan Just Schuchart, who worked with Bressan from at least 1719. Bressan had a sufficiently large room to put on several public exhibitions, including a viewing of one of Christopher Pinchbeck's musical machines, the 'Theatre of the Muses', in 1728.

Not much is known about his life. As part of the process of probate of his will a partial inventory of his goods was taken, giving a glimpse of his wider interests. In the rooms inventoried there is naturally much evidence of his instrument making but also indications that he had been a cultured person with an interest in the fine arts: a total of seventy-six pictures, prints, portraits and busts is itemized.

We know today of three flutes and some forty-five recorders by Bressan, of which nearly half are trebles (*cf* Fig 1). However, it is clear from the notes taken by the polymath James Talbot in the 1690s and from Bressan's inventory that he also made oboes and bassoons. The survival of such a number of recorders is due to their popularity among contemporary gentlemen amateurs.

The *St James Evening Post* of 6 May 1731 recorded Bressan's death, datelined Tournai, 20 April: 'On the 12th inst died here, and on the 16th was interred the Body of that celebrated Artist in making Flutes, Mr Bressan. He was taking a Tour thro the Austrian Netherlands and his loss is greatly regretted as well by all Lovers of Music, as by his inconsolable widow and three children (a son and two daughters) who reside in Somerset House London.'

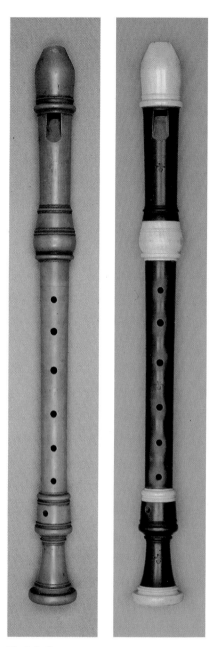

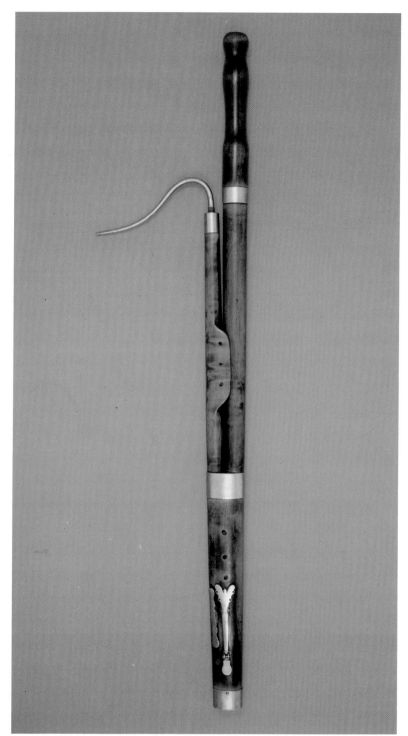

Fig 1 *Left*
A boxwood treble recorder by Peter
Bressan, London, stamped
PuI Bressan, first quarter eighteenth
century, length 19$\frac{15}{16}$in (50.6cm)
London £7,700($13,783). 7.IV.82
Right
A stained boxwood treble recorder
by Peter Bressan, London, stamped
PuI Bressan, first quarter eighteenth
century, length 19$\frac{9}{16}$in (49.7cm)
London £9,130($16,343). 9.X.81

Fig 2
A pearwood bassoon by Thomas Stanesby Senior, the boot stamped
T. Stanesby, the wing joint by Thomas Stanesby Junior, stamped *Stanesby
Iunior*, London, second quarter eighteenth century, length 47$\frac{7}{8}$in (121.6cm)
Reproduced courtesy of William Waterhouse

If Bressan was the successful foreigner setting up in Westminster, outside the City's jurisdiction, the Thomas Stanesbys, father and son, represented English orthodoxy, working in the City and coming from a clear line of master and apprentice in the Turners' Company back to the start of their surviving records in 1605. This line included Pepys's pipe maker Samuel Drumblebee and three other flute makers, Thomas Garret, William Smith and Joseph Bradbury.

Thomas Stanesby Senior was born in Derbyshire in 1668 and is thus the contemporary of Bressan. He was apprenticed to Thomas Garret in January 1682 and became free in 1691. He set up in Stonecutter Street in the parish of St Bride's, Fleet Street and lived all his working life there in a modest establishment of rateable value £9, compared with Bressan's £60. He married and had three children who survived infancy. Thomas Stanesby Junior was baptized on Christmas Day 1692 and, in 1706, he was apprenticed to his father. The father died in 1734, leaving his son all his pattern instruments and working tools. His surviving instruments include eight recorders, five oboes and the major part of a bassoon (Fig 2).

More is known about Stanesby Junior. He presumably set up in his own premises on reaching his majority. These were near Temple Bar in Fleet Street (cf Fig 3), and he spent his working life there. Curiously, he did not take the freedom of the Turners' Company until 1728, fifteen years after he was entitled to do so, but thereafter he involved himself in the life of the Company, becoming Master in 1739 and 1740. His business was successful and in 1727-28 he invested in £800 worth of 3 percent annuities, later adding £700 to this. He married, but his wife died young and without children. In 1743 he took on an apprentice called Caleb Gedney, who was to inherit Stanesby's working tools, materials and unfinished work, on condition that he married Stanesby's servant.

Sir John Hawkins in *A General History of the Science and Practice of Music* (1776) illustrates Stanesby's broader involvement with woodwind instruments. He records that he was interested in their history and studied seventeenth-century authorities. Following one of these, Mersenne, he made a racket, however, 'by reason of its closeness the interior parts imbibed and retained the moisture of the breath, [and] the ducts dilated and broke. In short the whole blew up.' In the 1730s, Stanesby published a plea for the tenor recorder, at a time when the interest of amateurs was moving towards flutes, and he was experimenting with flutes of extended downward range at the same period, according to a newspaper advertisement published by Gedney in 1756. Of his surviving instruments (cf Fig 4) twelve are recorders, twenty-seven flutes, three oboes and two bassoons: a noticeably different ratio of flutes to recorders from that of his father and Bressan in the previous generation.

He died in 1752, leaving £1,600 in 3 percent annuities. Of this, £1,000 was left to Mrs Browne 'who now lives with me'. She died within a month and a wrangle developed between one Thomas Browne, who claimed to have married her in the Crowne Tavern, Ludgate Hill, in 1734, and her brother. The brother won, and as part of the process a partial inventory was taken, revealing that Stanesby's premises had been largely over the Temple Exchange Coffee House, which Mrs Browne ran. Gedney married Stanesby's servant and carried on the business, but died aged only forty in 1769.

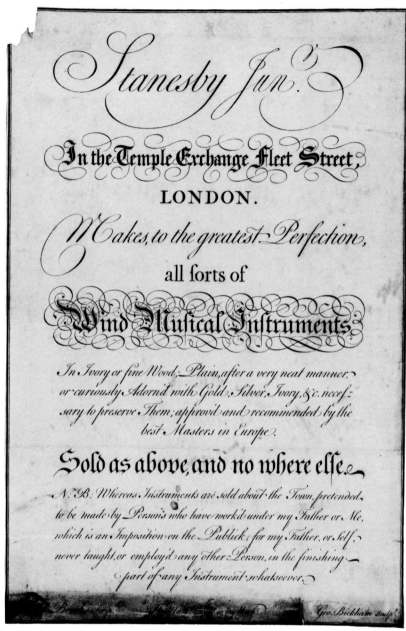

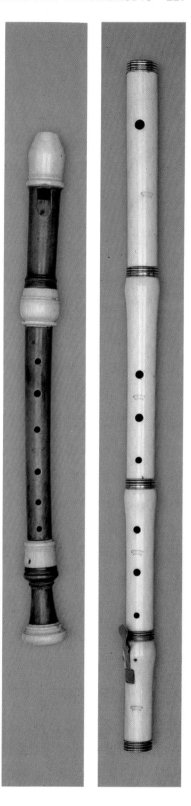

Fig 3
The trade card of Thomas Stanesby Junior, incorporating his maker's mark
and giving his address, 10½in by 7⅛in (26.7cm by 18cm)
Reproduced courtesy of the British Museum, London

Fig 4 *Near right*
A stained boxwood treble recorder by Thomas Stanesby Junior, London,
stamped *Stanesby Iunior*, second quarter eighteenth century,
length 19½in (49.5cm)
London £4,620 ($8,270). 9.X.81
Far right
A one-keyed ivory flute by Thomas Stanesby Junior, London, stamped *Stanesby
Iunior*, second quarter eighteenth century, sounding length 21¾in (55.2cm)
London £15,400 ($27,566). 9.X.81
From the collection of the late E. O. Pogson

Furniture and tapestries

A Federal painted pine blanket chest, Connecticut, *circa* 1825, width 4ft 1½in (125.7cm)
New York $40,700 (£22,737). 14.XI.81
From the Howard and Jean Lipman Collection, property of the Museum of American Folk Art,
New York

A Queen Anne walnut and maple flat-top highboy, North Shore, Massachusetts, 1720–40, height 5ft 8in
(172.7cm)
New York $209,000 (£116,760). 30.I.82
From the collection of the late Joseph H. Hirshhorn

A companion lowboy was sold with this piece

A Federal painted and gilt-ash lyre-back open armchair, Philadelphia, 1785–90
New York $26,400 (£14,749). 30.I.82

This chair was originally one of a set of twelve belonging to George Washington, listed by him in an inventory of 1797

A George II burr-walnut armchair by Giles Grendey, *circa* 1740
New York $66,000 (£36,872). 21.XI.81

One of a pair of George III gilt-wood side chairs in the manner
of John Linnell, *circa* 1770
London £18,150 ($32,489). 16.VII.82

A George III pembroke table with pen-work decoration, *circa* 1780, width 3ft $\frac{1}{4}$in (92cm)
London £10,450 ($18,706). 28.V.82

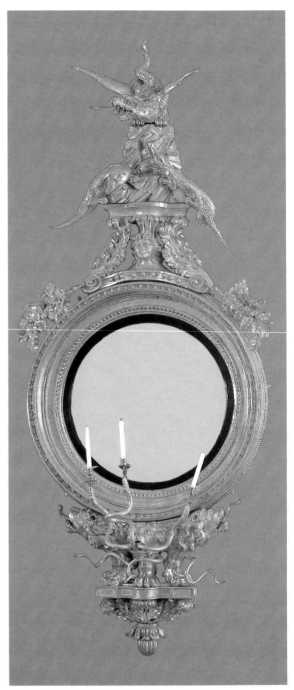

One of a pair of George II carved gilt-wood pier glasses in
the manner of John Linnell, *circa* 1755, height 9ft (274.3cm)
New York $110,000(£61,453). 17.IV.82
From the collection of the Hon and Mrs Walter
H. Annenberg

One of a pair of Regency carved gilt-wood girandoles,
circa 1815, height 9ft 10in (299.5cm)
Los Angeles $198,000(£110,615). 1.III.82

One of two Louis XIV gilt-bronze-mounted brass, pewter and tortoiseshell-inlaid coffers-on-stands by André-Charles Boulle, height 5ft 1in (155cm). Sold by private treaty

This coffer was probably made for the Grand Dauphin's apartments at Versailles, *circa* 1684, and is perhaps that recorded in an inventory of 1689. The second coffer may have been made for him, *circa* 1700, when he moved to Meudon

A pair of Louis XVI boulle pedestals, *circa* 1785, height 3ft 6in (106.7cm)
London £57,200 ($102,388). 25.VI.82

Opposite
A Louis XIV gilt-bronze-mounted brass and tortoiseshell-inlaid side table by André-Charles Boulle, width 3ft 10⅞in (119cm)
Monte Carlo FF 2,442,000 (£222,810:$398,830). 14.VI.82

This table corresponds closely to a print, plate 5, in the *Nouveaux Deisseins de Meubles et Ouvrages de Bronze et de Marqueterie inventés et gravés par André-Charles Boulle chez Mariette* and is similar to a drawing in the Musée des Arts Décoratifs, Paris (see black and white illustration), which is attributed to Boulle

Reproduced courtesy of
the Musée des Arts
Décoratifs, Paris

A Louis XV gilt–bronze–mounted satinwood and amaranth parquetry commode, stamped *J.F.Oeben*, *circa* 1760, width 5ft 6⅛in (168cm)
Monte Carlo FF 1,098,900 (£100,265:$179,474). 14.VI.82

Jean-François Oeben was *ébéniste du roi* between 1754 and 1763

A Louis XVI gilt-bronze-mounted mahogany commode by Jean-Henri Riesener, width 5ft 5in (165cm)
Monte Carlo FF 888,000 (£81,022:$145,029). 14.VI.82

Jean-Henri Riesener was *ébéniste du roi* between 1774 and 1785

A Rococo parcel-gilt fruitwood and walnut marquetry bureau cabinet, South
German or Austrian, *circa* 1740, height 10ft 2in (309.8cm)
Los Angeles $88,000 (£49,162). 4.XI.81

A Flemish gilt-metal-mounted walnut cabinet on a gilt-wood stand, second half seventeenth century, height 7ft 6in (228.5cm)
London £27,500 ($49,225). 23.IV.82

One of a pair of English gilt-bronze-mounted boulle side cabinets, *circa* 1880,
height 4ft 9⅛in (145cm)
London £27,500 ($49,225). 18.VI.82

These cabinets are modelled upon a pair by André-Charles Boulle in the Wallace Collection, London

A pair of English gilt-bronze and malachite-mounted marquetry cabinets, *circa* 1865, height of each
6ft 6¾in (199.8cm)
London £14,850 ($26,582). 16.XII.81

Among the woods used in this pair of cabinets are pear, chestnut, holly, sycamore, amboyna,
purpleheart, box and walnut

A French thuyawood mechanical writing cabinet, signed *Montagnot*, Lyons, *circa* 1850,
width 6ft 6½in (200cm)
London £33,000 ($59,070). 18.VI.82

It took eleven years to make this writing cabinet, and its thirty-five drawers and nine doors are
operated by twelve separate mechanisms

A French gilt-bronze-mounted kingwood display cabinet, signed *F.Linke*, the bronze sculpture by
Léon Message, height 12ft 6in (381cm)
Monte Carlo FF 888,000 (£81,022:$145,029). 25.X.81

This cabinet was made for the Paris Exposition Universelle of 1900

A Gothic *millefleurs* tapestry of serfs and villeins, probably Tournai, *circa* 1470,
10ft 5¼in by 10ft 5¼in (318cm by 318cm)
Monte Carlo FF1,554,000 (£141,788:$253,801). 7.II.82

A Franco-Flemish tapestry of the vintage, probably Tournai, *circa* 1500, 10ft 11½in by 11ft 2in
(334cm by 340cm)
Monte Carlo FF 888,000 (£81,022:$145,029). 7.II.82

A Louis XVI Gobelins tapestry, *Le repas de Sancho dans l'île de Barataria*, by Michel Audran, signed and dated *1772*, from a series of four tapestries depicting scenes from Cervantes's *Don Quixote* after Charles Coypel, 12ft 1½in by 16ft 5in (370cm by 500cm)
Monte Carlo FF 3,663,000 (£334,215: $598,245). 14.VI.82
From the Habsburg Collection

These four tapestries were presented by Louis XVI to his brother and sister-in-law, the Duke and Duchess of Saxe-Teschen in 1786. They formed part of the eighth series of *Don Quixote* tapestries to be produced by the Gobelins factory after Coypel's designs, which had first been copied in 1717

A wallpaper log-book from the Maison Réveillon
Monte Carlo FF 122,100 (£11,141:$19,942). 8.II.82
From the collection of the Maison Follot; and now in the Musée des Arts Décoratifs, Paris

The success of Jean-Baptiste Réveillon between 1760 and 1789 coincides with the golden age of wallpaper. He made use of all the latest developments: the sticking together of sheets to make a roll, high-quality vellum-like papers, block-printing *à la frappe* and the finest colours. Above all, he raised the status of wallpaper from an industry to an art by commissioning the best artists of the period, some of whom were associated with the Gobelins tapestry works: artists like Cietti, Jean-Baptiste Fay, Huet, Lavallée-Poussin, Prieur and Boucher designed for him the famous *panneaux arabesques* as well as imitations of *toiles de jouy* and *toiles de l'Inde*. His Paris factory in the Faubourg Saint-Antoine could accommodate three hundred workers, whom he organized into three grades according to their ability. Here, he produced three kinds of papers, aimed at suiting both the rich and the less wealthy. The very expensive ones might require as many as eighty blocks and were sometimes as costly as a Gobelins tapestry. The middle range for the bourgeoisie required seven or eight blocks, and finally the most ordinary papers were of one colour, intended for common use. His talents as an enterprising businessman were recognized by Louis XVI who conferred upon his firm the title of *manufacture royale* in 1784. The business ended abruptly on 28 April 1789 when the factory was destroyed by the mob, who had been led to believe that Réveillon was grossly underpaying his employees

Silver

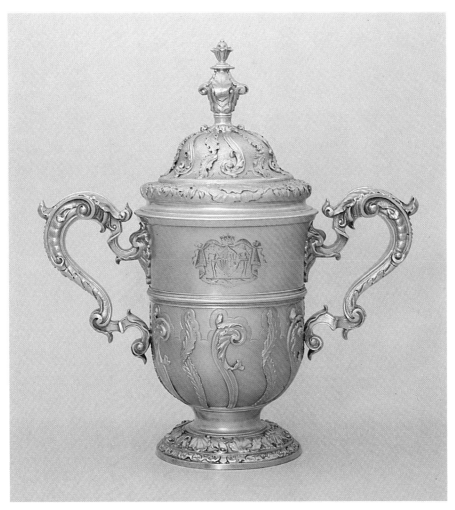

A George II silver-gilt cup and cover, maker's mark of Thomas Farren, London, 1740, height 13in (33cm)
London £9,350 ($16,737). 19.XI.81

Thomas Farren entered his first mark in 1707 and was subordinate goldsmith to the king between 1723 and 1742

The Great Mace of the Corporation of Athy,
maker's mark of John Williamson, Dublin,
1746, height 46¼in (117.5cm)
London £17,050 ($30,520). 18.III.82

This mace was presented to the Irish borough of
Athy, County Kildare, by James, 20th Earl of
Kildare in 1746. There are approximately one
hundred Great Maces extant, ranging in date
from the seventeenth to the twentieth centuries.
The majority are still in the possession of the
relevant corporations

A George III silver-gilt jug and cover, maker's mark of Paul Storr, London, 1799,
height $13\frac{1}{4}$in (33.6cm)
London £23,100 ($41,349). 18.III.82

The arms are those of George III and of Thomas, 7th Earl of Elgin. Elgin was
ambassador to Constantinople from 1799 to 1803 and instigated the removal of
the frieze from the Parthenon. The 'Elgin marbles' were subsequently purchased
by Act of Parliament for the British Museum in 1816. The 10th Earl of Elgin sold
this jug for £48 8s in 1926

A pair of silver-gilt bowls and covers, *circa* 1680, diameter of each 5$\frac{1}{4}$in (13.5cm)
London £5,280 ($9,451). 19.VII.82

A pair of George II tea caddies and a sugar box, maker's mark of Paul de Lamerie, London, 1738,
height of each 4$\frac{1}{4}$in (10.8cm)
London £35,200 ($63,008). 18.III.82

A pair of George III wine coolers, maker's mark of Joseph Preedy, London, 1802, height of each 11$\frac{1}{8}$in (28.2cm)
London £11,440 ($20,478). 19.VII.82

A pair of salt cellars, maker's mark of Robert Garrard for R. & S. Garrard & Co, London, 1857,
height of each 5¾in (14.5cm)
London £4,400 ($7,876). 17.XII.81

Opposite
A set of four George III candlesticks, maker's mark of John Carter, London, 1774,
height of each 10¾in (27.3cm)
London £9,680 ($17,327). 19.XI.81

A soup tureen with cover and stand, maker's mark of Engelbart Joosten, The Hague, 1763, width of stand 19¾in (50cm)
Amsterdam DFl 180,960 (£38,916 : $69,660). 19.XI.81

Now in the Rijksmuseum, Amsterdam

Opposite
A parcel-gilt shield of the Münster Goldsmiths' Guild, maker's mark of Hermann Potthof, Münster, 1613, height 6½in (16.5cm)
Geneva SFr 286,000 (£79,888 : $143,000). 6.V.82

Hermann Potthof was apprenticed to the Nuremberg goldsmith, Bartel Jamnitzer, but the composition and fine chasing of this shield suggest the style of Anton Eisenhoit of Warburg, who died in 1603: the chasing was perhaps put out to one of his pupils. In the centre are the arms of the Münster Goldsmiths' Guild, flanked by the arms or devices of sixteen master goldsmiths. The shield was probably fixed to a cloth covering the coffin of a deceased master at the burial service, following the custom of Dutch goldsmiths' guilds

A two-handled bowl, maker's mark of Benjamin Wynkoop, New York, *circa* 1707, width 11in (27.9cm)
New York $121,000 (£67,598). 17.XI.81

This bowl bears the initials of Nicholas Roosevelt and his wife, Hillitje, Dutch settlers in New York.
Roosevelt, a 'bolter' by profession, was made a freeman in 1698 and served several times as an
alderman. Fewer than twenty bowls of this type are known and they reflect the influence of Dutch
craftsmanship in the former New Netherlands

A teapot, maker's mark of Myer Myers, New York, *circa* 1750–60, height $7\frac{1}{4}$ in (18.4cm)
New York $63,250 (£35,335). 27.I.82
From the collection of the late William Floyd II

The initials on this teapot are those of Nicholas and Tabatha Floyd, parents of William Floyd, who was among the signatories of the American Declaration of Independence

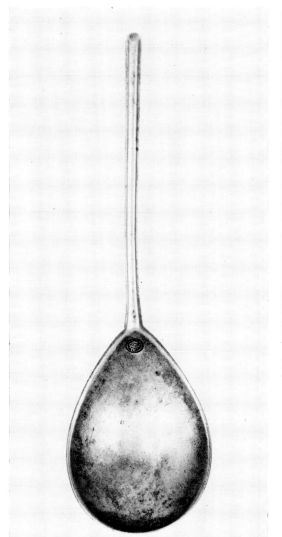

An ashtray, maker's mark of James Barclay Hennell for R. Hennell & Son, London, 1884, diameter 4in (10.1cm)
London £253 ($453). 17.XII.81

An Edward IV slip top spoon, London, *circa* 1465, length 6½in (16.5cm)
London £10,120 ($18,115). 19.XI.81

This may be the earliest known slip top spoon

Right
An Irish George III silver-mounted wood Freedom box, *circa* 1795, width 3in (7.6cm)
London £3,190 ($5,710). 19.XI.81

The box is inscribed: *Christmas Assembly 1795. The Freedom of the City of Dublin was ordered to be presented in this Box to the Honble Thos. Packenham Captn. of his Majestys Ship the Invincible for his noble & gallant Conduct in the Glorious Action of the 1st June 1794.* On this date the English had scattered a French fleet

A 'Japanese' tray, maker's mark of Tiffany & Co, New York, *circa* 1880, width 23in (58.4cm)
$7,700 (£4,302)
From left to right
A 'Japanese' coffee pot, maker's mark of Tiffany & Co, New York, *circa* 1877, height 7in (17.8cm)
$1,870 (£1,045)
A 'Japanese' two-handled sugar bowl and cover, maker's mark of Tiffany & Co, New York, *circa* 1877,
height 5½in (14cm)
$2,860 (£1,598)
A 'Japanese' coffee pot, maker's mark of Tiffany & Co, New York, *circa* 1877, height 11in (27.9cm)
$4,840 (£2,704)

The silver illustrated on this page was sold in New York on 21 November 1981

European ceramics

From left to right
A Chelsea 'botanical' saucer-dish, marked with red anchor, *circa* 1754–56, diameter 8in (20.3cm)
£4,840 ($8,664)
A Chelsea 'botanical' dish, marked with red anchor, *circa* 1754–56, diameter 14⅝in (37.2cm)
£4,950 ($8,861)
A Chelsea 'botanical' saucer-dish, marked with red anchor, *circa* 1754–56, diameter 8in (20.3cm)
£4,840 ($8,664)

From left to right
A Chelsea 'botanical' dish, marked with red anchor, *circa* 1754–56, diameter 16¾in (42.5cm)
£5,280 ($9,451)
A Chelsea 'botanical' dish, marked with red anchor, *circa* 1754–56, diameter 14in (35.5cm)
£6,600 ($11,814)

The porcelain illustrated on this page was sold in London on 16 July 1982

The Wedgwood 'Sneyd' copy of the Portland Vase, blue jasper decorated in low white and black relief, *circa* 1797, height $10\frac{3}{8}$ in (26.3cm)
London £29,700 ($53,163). 20.X.81

'A $2 candy dish'

Letitia Roberts

'$2 CANDY DISH BRINGS $60,000 AT NEW YORK AUCTION' trumpeted American newspaper headlines on 29 January 1982. The 'candy dish' was, in fact, a Bonnin and Morris sweetmeat stand (see opposite) – the third recorded piece of this form, and one of less than twenty known extant pieces from this obscure factory. The owner had bought it unwittingly for $2 at a 'tag sale' held by a friend but, by the time he parted with it, he had deduced its origin from the 'P' mark in underglaze-blue under one shell: the factory had announced in 1771 that its mark would be a letter 'S', perhaps for Southwark, the factory site in Philadelphia, but surviving marked pieces bear either a 'P', probably for Philadelphia, or a 'Z'.

The Bonnin and Morris factory was America's first and only eighteenth-century porcelain factory. It had propitious beginnings under the protection of the Non-importation Act of 1769, a tariff act restricting British imports; but the act was repealed in 1770 and cheaper wares, imported by the East India Company, flooded the market, ultimately forcing the factory to close.

One of the factory's principals, Gousse Bonnin, was born about 1741, the son of a prosperous Antigua merchant, and educated at Eton. In 1766, he married Dorothy Palmer, the daughter of a baronet, and two years later he sailed for America with his wife and infant son. He landed in Philadelphia, and applied to London for a patent to manufacture black lead and clay crucibles. Before the factory was fully operative, however, the impulsive Bonnin had formed a partnership with his friend George Anthony Morris to open an 'American China Manufactory'.

Morris was born about 1742–45 into a prominent family in Philadelphia. It was probably Morris's family and influential friends, with some reluctant support from Bonnin's father-in-law, who financed the factory on a plot of Morris family land. It was announced in the *Pennsylvania Chronicle* on 1 January 1770 under the headline 'NEW CHINA WARE' that 'the proprietors . . . have proved . . . that the clays of America are productive of as good porcelain as any heretofore manufactured at . . . Bow, near London'.

The first wares did not appear until 24 December 1770. These soft-paste porcelains were decorated primarily in underglaze-blue, by brush and transfer print. Advertisements the following September indicated that colourfully enamelled wares were to be made available, but no examples have been recorded, other than a few shards in underglaze-red, discovered during the 1967 excavation of the factory site.

The factory offered 'compleat sets for the dining and tea table', including dinner plates, sauceboats and bowls in several sizes, a variety of standard tea wares, open-

A Bonnin and Morris sweetmeat stand, marked *P* in underglaze-blue, Philadelphia, 1771–72, height 5⅛in (13cm)
New York $66,000(£36,872). 28.I.82

work fruit baskets, patty pans, shell-shaped pickle dishes, sweetmeat stands or 'pickle stands' (the most expensive of the products at fifteen shillings each), and eventually 'sets of Dressing Boxes for the Toilet', of which no examples are known.

By the summer of 1771, the expense of production, the dissatisfaction of the homesick, underpaid workers imported from Staffordshire, and the insurmountable competition of cheaper and better products from abroad, had all conspired against the factory's success. A charitable lottery and patriotic broadsides in the *Pennsylvania Gazette* did little to arrest its decline. Production continued until about September 1772, when Bonnin decided to close to avoid bankruptcy. He returned to England in 1773 and Morris died that same year in North Carolina.

It was over half a century before Joseph Hemphill and William Ellis Tucker opened America's next short-lived china factory and almost fifty more years before porcelain manufacture could be considered a serious industry in America. In that perspective, the little colonial enterprise of Bonnin and Morris seems all the more remarkable.

A Meissen 'Kakiemon' dish, marked with crossed swords in blue enamel, *circa* 1730,
diameter $9\frac{5}{8}$in (24.3cm)
London £9,570 ($17,130). 29.VI.82

Opposite, above
A Böttger stoneware teapot and cover, marked with impressed crescent, 1710–20,
height $4\frac{1}{8}$in (10.5cm)
Zurich SFr 52,800 (£14,749:$26,401). 2.XII.81

Opposite, below
A Böttger stoneware tankard with silver mounts, 1710–15, height $4\frac{7}{8}$in (12.5cm)
Zurich SFr 57,200 (£15,978:$28,601). 2.XII.81

A Nymphenburg figure of Octavio from the *Commedia dell'arte*, modelled by Franz Anton Bustelli, marked with impressed shield and incised *B/I, circa* 1755–60, height 8⅛in (20.5cm)
Zurich SFr 50,600 (£14,134:$25,300). 2.XII.81

A Nymphenburg figure of Leda from the *Commedia dell'arte*, modelled by Franz Anton Bustelli, marked with incised *O, circa* 1765, height 8⅛in (20.6cm)
Zurich SFr 44,000 (£12,291:$22,001). 2.XII.81

Opposite
A Meissen figure of Columbine from the *Commedia dell'arte*, modelled by Johann Joachim Kaendler, *circa* 1735–40, height 7⅝in (19.5cm)
Zurich SFr 88,000 (£24,581:$44,000). 2.XII.81

From left to right
A Meissen armorial chocolate cup and saucer, with the arms of Elector Clemens August of Cologne, marked with crossed swords in underglaze-blue, dated *1735*
London £12,100 ($21,659). 29.VI.82
A Meissen armorial chocolate cup and saucer, marked with crossed swords in underglaze-blue, *circa* 1735
London £3,300 ($5,907). 29.VI.82

A Meissen armorial cup and saucer, with the arms of Edward Howard, 9th Duke of Norfolk, impaling those of his wife, Mary Blount of Blagdon, marked with crossed swords in underglaze-blue, *circa* 1732–39
Zurich SFr 27,500 (£7,682:$13,751). 2.XII.81

A pair of Frankenthal figures of Oceanus and Thetis, modelled by Konrad Linck, each marked with
crowned *CT*, *circa* 1765, height of each 11$\frac{1}{4}$in (28.5cm); 10$\frac{1}{4}$in (26cm)
New York $55,000 (£30,726). 22.IV.82
From the collection of Mrs H. Graves Terwilliger

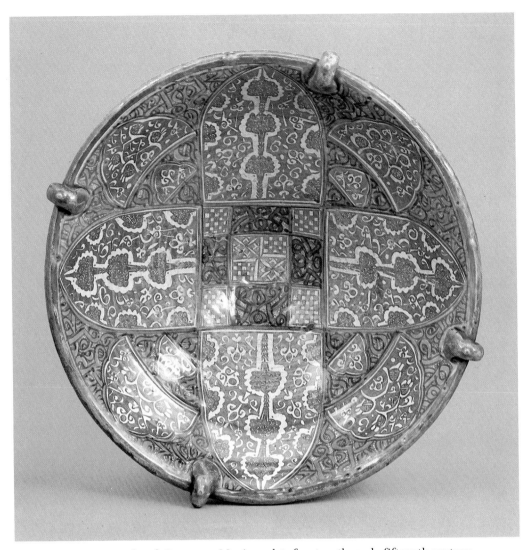

An Hispano-Moresque bowl, Paterna or Manisses, late fourteenth–early fifteenth century,
diameter 18⅛in (46cm)
London £18,700($33,473). 8.XII.81

A Dutch Delft plate, painted by Frederik van Frytom, late seventeenth century,
diameter $9\frac{7}{8}$in (25cm)
London £5,500($9,845). 8.XII.81

Frederik van Frytom (1632–1702) was one of the most distinguished painters working in Delft
and one of the few whose work can be identified with certainty

A polychrome tile, Rotterdam,
early seventeenth century
Amsterdam DF1 12,760 (£2,744:$4,912).
18.XI.81
From the collection of F. Leerink

A polychrome tile, Rotterdam,
early seventeenth century
Amsterdam DF1 10,904 (£2,345:$4,198).
18.XI.81
From the collection of F. Leerink

A Strasbourg faïence partridge tureen and cover, *circa* 1750–54, length 7½in (19cm)
London £9,900 ($17,721). 25.V.82

A Brussels faïence fish tureen and cover, marked *Bn 2* on base and *Bn 3* inside cover, Wittensburg and Mombaeus factory, mid eighteenth century, length 19¼in (49cm)
London £5,720 ($10,239). 25.V.82

From left to right
A Frankfurt faïence polychrome *Enghalskrug* with silver-gilt mounts, 1680–90, height $9\frac{1}{2}$in (24.1cm)
New York $28,600 (£15,978). 22.IV.82
A German faïence polychrome Hausmaler *Enghalskrug* with pewter mounts, painted by
Bartholomäus Seuter, Augsburg, *circa* 1720, height $9\frac{7}{8}$in (25.1cm)
New York $26,400 (£14,749). 22.IV.82

A pair of gilt-bronze-mounted 'Vienna' vases and covers, third quarter nineteenth century,
height of each 43½in (110.4cm)
London £12,650 ($22,644). 12.XI.81

A Berlin plaque, painted by F. Wagner after Hans Makart, signed, marked with impressed sceptre and *K.P.M.*, *circa* 1880, $11\frac{3}{4}$in by $21\frac{5}{8}$in (30cm by 55cm)
London £11,000 ($19,690). 12.XI.81

A Royal Worcester pierced court shoe by George Owen, signed, marked with printed crowned circle and date code for 1919, length $7\frac{3}{4}$in (19.5cm) London £4,290 ($7,679). 18.III.82

Three pieces from a Coalport dessert service, painted by F. H. Chivers, each signed and marked with printed crown, *circa* 1910, diameter of plate $8\frac{7}{8}$in (22.7cm)
London £2,035 ($3,643). 8.X.81

Left and right
A pair of Wedgwood Fairyland Lustre vases, each marked with printed urn, 1920–30, height of each 11in (28cm)
London £2,090 ($3,741). 18.III.82
Centre
A Wedgwood Fairyland Lustre punch bowl, marked with printed urn, 1920–30, diameter $11\frac{3}{8}$in (28.8cm)
London £880 ($1,575). 18.III.82

Glass
and
paperweights

A St Louis turnip weight,
diameter $3\frac{1}{8}$in (8cm)
$16,500 (£9,218)

A St Louis concentric-millefiori
piedouche weight, dated *1848*,
diameter $3\frac{1}{4}$in (8.2cm)
$7,700 (£4,302)

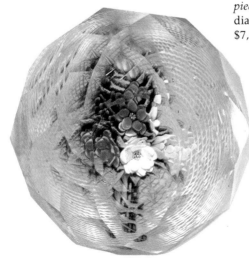

A New England faceted flat-bouquet weight,
probably by Nicholas Lutz, diameter $3\frac{3}{4}$in (9.5cm)
$15,400 (£8,603)

A lily-of-the-valley weight,
diameter $3\frac{3}{8}$in (8.5cm)
$47,300 (£26,425)

The paperweights illustrated on this page are from the collection of Wayne T. Moses and were sold
in New York on 18 May 1982

A bottle engraved by Willem van Heemskerk, signed, inscribed *LYD EN MYD/VLYT BEDYT* and dated *1689*, height 13in (33cm)
London £6,380($11,420). 21.X.81

The Helfried Krug Collection –
a private museum of European glass

Walter Spiegl

The Krug Collection was formed in the relatively short span of twenty years, becoming in volume and quality one of the most comprehensive collections of European glass in private possession. There were over 790 specimens in the collection, the majority being of European origin; mostly Venetian, *façon de Venise*, Bohemian, Silesian and German. As a whole, the collection illustrated glassmaking and glass decoration through 400 years of development.

In the middle of the fifteenth century, a type of glass called *waldglas* was commonly used by glassmakers in northern Europe. This glass is greenish or yellowish in colour, as a result of iron impurities in the sand used for manufacture and of the potash fluxing agent, made from the ashes of beech wood. An early *waldglas* vessel from the Krug Collection is a Gothic-type green flask of double conical form (Fig 1).

At about the same time, Italy was experiencing a revival of glassmaking. Sands of better quality and the use of Mediterranean soda ash as a fluxing agent enabled Venetian glassmakers to produce a fragile colourless glass resembling rock crystal, which they called *cristallo* (Fig 3). This *cristallo* was occasionally decorated with blue, green or purple glass applications. There is a further distinction to be drawn between the style of Italian drinking glasses and those from northern Europe, as may be seen by comparing Figure 3 with a typical northern European shape, Figure 2. Venetian vessels imitated forms used by Renaissance goldsmiths, reaching a peak of elegance in the late sixteenth and early seventeenth centuries.

In northern Europe there rapidly grew up a demand for Venetian glass and this led to the foundation of glasshouses operated by Italian glassmakers north of the Alps. One of the earliest of these was at Hall-in-Tyrol, and the tazza with diamond-engraved double-headed eagles flanked by floral motifs from the Krug Collection is a beautiful example of *façon-de-Venise* glass produced there (Fig 4). Under northern European influence, new forms of vessel were created and produced in Germany and the Netherlands, using Venetian-style decorative techniques intrinsic to the glass itself and carried out in the glasshouse. Coloured glass scrolls and nipped decoration were applied to serpent stems of coiled incised tubing. One outstanding glass from the collection illustrates the practice of imbedding threads or twisted strands of white glass in the *cristallo*, to produce what is sometimes known as filigree glass (Fig 5).

Fig 1
A German *waldglas* flask, fifteenth century,
height 6⅝in (17cm)
London £8,800 ($15,752). 7.XII.81
From the collection of Mr and Mrs Helfried Krug

Fig 2
A Netherlandish *Roemer*, mid seventeenth century,
height 10¼in (26cm)
London £2,090 ($3,741). 7.XII.81
From the collection of Mr and Mrs Helfried Krug

However, glass *à la façon de Venise* did not completely displace the German tradition. The *Roemer*, first mentioned in Cologne documents from the second half of the fifteenth century, was still considered the ideal wine glass in Germany: and the seventeenth-century *Roemers* in the Krug Collection remind one of the 30,000 *Roemers* which the Laubach glasshouse in Hesse produced for Tynnes Jacobs of Amsterdam in 1685. *Roemers* of many types and sizes were made in Holland itself at this time (Fig 2), sometimes engraved in diamond point with exquisite calligraphy.

Until about 1550 glasses with enamel decoration had to be imported from Italy but, by the second half of the sixteenth century, German glasshouses had advanced technically and were able to produce glass suitable for enamelling. Enamel colours were

Fig 3
A Venetian enamelled and gilt *cristallo*
goblet, *circa* 1500, height $7\frac{1}{8}$in (18cm)
London £6,600 ($11,814). 7.XII.81
From the collection of Mr and Mrs
Helfried Krug

Fig 4
A *façon-de-Venise* diamond-engraved tazza,
Hall-in-Tyrol, *circa* 1580, height $5\frac{7}{8}$in (15cm)
London £13,750. 7.VII.81
From the collection of Mr and Mrs
Helfried Krug

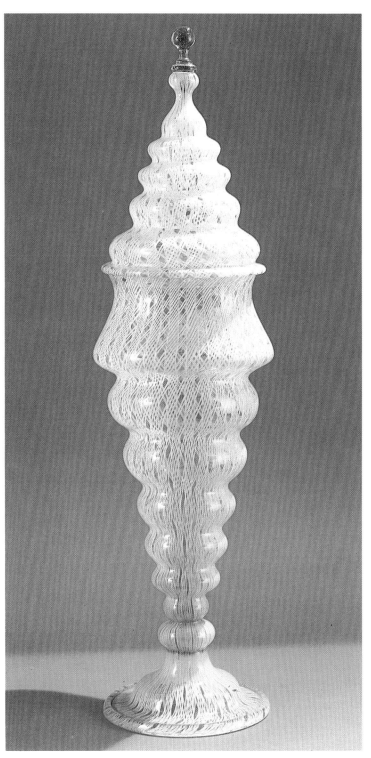

Fig 5
A *façon-de-Venise* filigree-glass goblet and cover, South
Netherlands, late sixteenth–early seventeenth century,
height $17\frac{7}{8}$in (45.5cm)
London £16,500. 7.VII.81
From the collection of Mr and Mrs Helfried Krug

Fig 6
A Bohemian enamelled and gilt *Reichsadlerhumpen*, signed
G.P., inscribed and dated *1573*, height 11¼in (28.5cm)
London £16,500($29,535). 7.XII.81
From the collection of Mr and Mrs Helfried Krug

Fig 7
A Saxon enamelled *Passglas*, inscribed, early
eighteenth century, height 10⅜in (26.5cm)
London £8,800($15,752). 7.XII.81
From the collection of Mr and Mrs Helfried Krug

based on powdered glass, with metallic oxides added as colouring agents, and were available in a rich palette. The use of enamel colours, *schwarzlot* and gold became widespread in the last third of the sixteenth century continuing well into the eighteenth, when opaque white *milchglas* became popular as a cheap surrogate for porcelain. The Krug Collection was especially rich in German and Bohemian enamelled glass and included some excellent specimens, such as a very early Bohemian *Reichsadlerhumpen* dated *1573* (Fig 6). A Saxon *Passglas* with a lobster painted in red and black is a fine example of later German enamelling (Fig 7).

In the early seventeenth century, a new form of glass decoration arose, influenced by the cutting and wheel engraving of hardstones. Caspar Lehmann, a German gem engraver who worked for Emperor Rudolf II in Prague from 1588, was the first to master the transposition of hardstone engraving to glass. His earliest known engraved glasses are a beaker signed and dated *1605*, and a portrait plaque which was either made in Prague, in 1602, or in Dresden, in 1606. Lehmann's pupil in Prague, Georg Schwanhardt, returned to his native Nuremberg in 1622, after his master's death, and became the first of the famous Schwanhardt dynasty of glass engravers. He established the high standard of Nuremberg glass for wheel-engraved decoration (*cf* Fig 10), which continued into the middle of the eighteenth century.

The earliest example of a Bohemian wheel-engraved glass in the Krug Collection was a beaker decorated with the four continents by the Master of the Koula Beaker, dating from the third quarter of the seventeenth century (Fig 8). It not only marks the revival of glass engraving after the end of the Thirty Years' War (1618–48), which had interrupted development after Lehmann's death, but also illustrates a new type of glass that had been invented in Bohemia.

Bohemian crystal glass has the hardness of rock crystal and keeps its brilliancy even when formed into thick-walled vessels. It is the latter property which distinguishes it from the fragile Italian *cristallo*. Bohemian crystal is a potash-lime glass. It is therefore lighter than glass containing lead and, although it does not have the excellent light-dispersing quality of English lead glass, its hardness and brilliancy make it an ideal material for wheel engraving and cutting.

There were two other early examples of Bohemian crystal-glass cutting in the collection (*cf* Fig 9). Both are engraved beakers with thumb-nail flutes and shallow circular concavities (printies), made with the grinding wheel commonly used for grinding away the pontil marks. By 1710–20, cutting had become a common means of decoration, and in the following decades it became the rule that every glass of distinction should be worked by the cutter before further decoration.

Bohemian crystal was widely used everywhere in Germany. The Potsdam glass-house, founded and operated by Johann Kunckel, employed some of the most talented decorators, among them Gottfried Spiller, who had come to Potsdam from Silesia with Martin Winter. Spiller's style can be seen on a mammoth goblet and cover bearing the arms of Elector Friedrich III of Brandenburg (Fig 11).

A late seventeenth-century crystal-glass goblet and cover from the workshop of Friedrich Winter, Martin's brother, was one of the most exceptional pieces in the Krug Collection (see *Art at Auction 1980–81*, p 233). It was produced in the Silesian mountain village of Hermsdorf and is decorated in *hochschnitt*, or high-relief carving,

Fig 8
A Bohemian beaker, probably wheel engraved
by the Master of the Koula Beaker, third quarter
seventeenth century, height 4½in (11.5cm)
London £4,400. 7.VII.81
From the collection of Mr and Mrs Helfried Krug

Fig 9
A Bohemian *tiefschnitt* portrait beaker of
Elector Johann Georg III of Saxony and with a
view of the Siege of Vienna, inscribed,
circa 1685, height 4⅛in (10.5cm)
London £3,300. 7.VII.81
From the collection of Mr and Mrs Helfried Krug

Fig 10
A portrait goblet of Paul Albrecht Rieter, wheel engraved by
Hermann Schwinger, inscribed, Nuremburg, *circa* 1682,
height 11⅝in (29.5cm)
London £17,050. 7.VII.81
From the collection of Mr and Mrs Helfried Krug

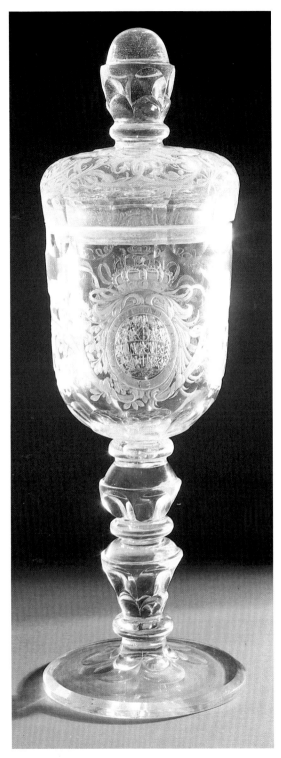

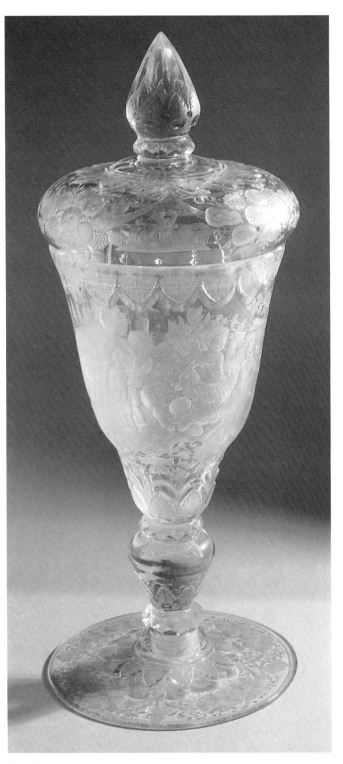

Fig 11
A goblet and cover decorated with the arms of
Elector Friedrich III of Brandenburg, by Gottfried
Spiller, Potsdam, 1688–1701, height 15⅞in (40.5cm)
London £19,800. 7.VII.81
From the collection of Mr and Mrs Helfried Krug

Fig 12
A Silesian wheel-engraved goblet and cover decorated with
Bacchic scenes, from the workshop of Friedrich Winter,
Hermsdorf, *circa* 1700–10, height 15⅜in (39cm)
London £31,900 ($57,101). 7.XII.81
From the collection of Mr and Mrs Helfried Krug

Fig 13 *From left to right*
A Bohemian *zwischengold* beaker, inscribed, *circa* 1730, height $3\frac{3}{8}$in (8.5cm). £1,650
A Bohemian *zwischengold* beaker, *circa* 1730, height $3\frac{7}{8}$in (10cm). £825
A Bohemian *zwischengold* beaker and cover, *circa* 1730, height $5\frac{1}{4}$in (13.5cm). £4,400
A Bohemian *zwischengold* beaker, *circa* 1730, height $3\frac{1}{8}$in (8cm). £880

The glasses illustrated above are from the collection of Mr and Mrs Helfried Krug and were sold in London on 7 July 1981

with Baroque ornament on a polished ground. Almost as remarkable is another goblet and cover from the same workshop, dating from the first decade of the eighteenth century and decorated with sparse *hochschnitt* decoration and Bacchic scenes in *mattschnitt*, or matt engraving (Fig 12).

Another group of glasses which illustrate the high skill and versatility of eighteenth-century glass decorators are the Bohemian *zwischengold* beakers and goblets. They are decorated in gold and silver foil, often heightened with coloured lacquers, encased between two walls of glass. The fifty-two specimens in the Krug Collection gave an impression of the vast variety of this elaborate technique (Fig 13).

Several examples from the collection of gold ruby glass and *milchglas*, and a rare Saxon amber-tinted marriage goblet, demonstrate the use of coloured glass in the eighteenth century. In general, however, coloured glass seems not to have been widely used, although the formulae for making it had been published by Kunckel in 1756. It was only in the second quarter of the nineteenth century, in the Biedermeier period, that higher technological standards made possible the industrialized production of transparent and opaque glasses in all the colours of precious stones.

One of the main aims of the Krugs was to assemble representative pieces from all the great European glassmaking centres. Thus, besides highlights such as the *hochschnitt* goblets, there were many more humble pieces. This comprehensive collection enabled the viewer to take in the breadth and invention, and the multitude of forms and techniques with which the glassmaker transforms his craft into art. It now joins the ranks of other famous collections to be dispersed in the saleroom, such as the Beck and Smith collections. So many pieces could not all be dispersed at once and next season will see the sale of the remaining German and nineteenth-century glasses.

Art Nouveau and Art Deco

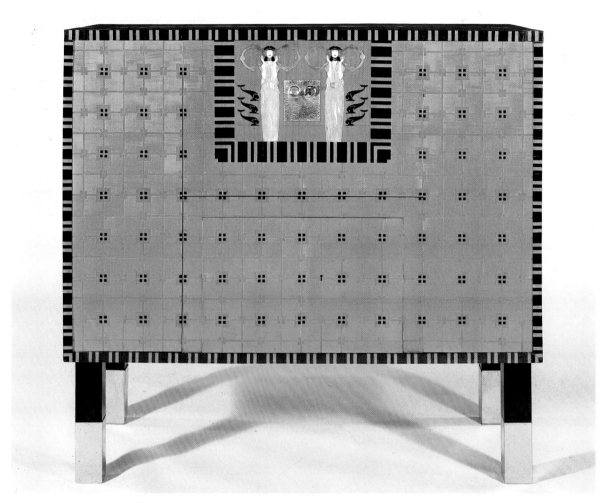

A Secessionist ivory, mother-of-pearl, ebony, elm and jacaranda-inlaid desk designed by Koloman Moser, Vienna, 1902, width 3ft 11$\frac{1}{4}$in (120cm)
Monte Carlo FF 1,665,000 (£151,916:$271,930). 19.IV.82

This desk was ordered in 1902 for the château of Charlottenlund, near Stockholm

An egg-shell lacquer dressing table and chair by Emile-Jacques Ruhlmann and Jean Dunand, Paris, 1927, height of dressing table 3ft 9¼in (115cm)
Monte Carlo FF 1,098,900 (£100,265:$179,474). 19.IV.82

A mahogany cabinet designed by Walter Gropius, 1913, height 6ft (183cm)
New York $24,200 (£13,520). 21.XI.81

A Tiffany Favrile glass vase, *circa* 1900,
height 14¼in (36.2cm)
New York $53,900(£30,112). 20.V.82
From the collection of the late Pauline Heilman

A lacquered metal vase by Jean Dunand, marked *Jean Dunand*,
Paris, *circa* 1925, height 9¼in (23.5cm)
Monte Carlo FF 81,030(£7,393:$13,233). 7.XII.81

A silver, bronze and enamel dish by René Lalique, stamped *Lalique*, *circa* 1900, diameter 8⅛in (20.5cm)
Monte Carlo FF 144,300(£13,166:$23,567). 7.XII.81

An ebony and willow-veneered writing cabinet designed by Charles Robert Ashbee, *circa* 1902,
height 4ft 5½in (136cm)
London £31,900($57,101). 10.XII.81

Above
A stoneware vase by Hans Coper, impressed *HC* seal, *circa* 1965, height 11¾in (30cm). £2,310 ($4,135)
Below, from left to right
A stoneware vase by Hans Coper, impressed *HC* seal, *circa* 1970, height 7⅜in (18.8cm). £528 ($945)

A black stoneware vase by Hans Coper, impressed *HC* seal, *circa* 1974, height 8in (20.5cm). £2,310 ($4,135)
A black stoneware vase by Hans Coper, impressed *HC* seal, *circa* 1974, height 7⅜in (18.7cm). £1,650 ($2,954)
A porcelain bottle-vase by Lucie Rie, impressed *LR* seal, *circa* 1970, height 10⅞in (27.7cm). £352 ($630)

The studio ceramics illustrated on this page were sold in London on 11 December 1981

Jewellery

Above
A sapphire and diamond tiara, nineteenth century. SFr 60,500 (£16,899:$30,249)
Below
A diamond tiara, nineteenth century. SFr 33,000 (£9,218:$16,500)

The jewellery illustrated on this page was sold in Geneva on 6 May 1982

An Art Deco gold, enamel, coral, jade and diamond mantel clock by Cartier, dated *3rd June 1926*
Geneva SFr 275,000 (£76,816:$137,501). 12.XI.81

Above
A ruby, emerald and diamond brooch. HK $77,000 (£7,476:$13,382)
Centre
An emerald and diamond ring. HK $20,350 (£1,976:$3,537)
Below
A ruby and diamond necklace. HK $330,000 (£32,039:$57,350)

The jewellery illustrated on this page was sold in Hong Kong on 23 November 1981

Above, from left to right
A turquoise and diamond brooch, *circa* 1830. £4,620($8,270)
A fancy coloured diamond brooch, *circa* 1800. £10,450($18,706)
Below, from left to right
A gold, ruby and diamond brooch from a demi-parure. £1,430($2,560)
A gold, enamel, pearl, sapphire and diamond Holbeinesque pendant and a pair of pendent earrings, *circa* 1870. £14,300($25,597)
An emerald and diamond brooch, first quarter nineteenth century. £2,090($3,741)

The jewellery illustrated on this page was sold in London on 24 September 1981

A *sarpesh* comprising a ruby, emerald, sapphire and diamond *jigha*, and a ruby, emerald and diamond *sarpate*, probably Bengal, mid eighteenth century
London £13,200 ($23,628). 22.IV.82

These jewels were originally owned by Admiral Charles Watson (1714–57) and were probably a gift from Alivardi Khan of Murshidabad

An emerald and diamond pendant, nineteenth century. Geneva SFr 242,000 (£67,598:$121,000). 12.XI.81

A diamond brooch, the fancy pink diamonds weighing 9.13 carats, mid nineteenth century. New York $396,000 (£221,229). 27.X.81 From the collection of the late Mrs Ernest Goldsmith

An emerald (approx 32 carats) and diamond brooch with detachable emerald drop (approx 23 carats), late nineteenth century. New York $99,000 (£55,307). 10.XII.81 From the collection of HRH, the Crown Princess of Yugoslavia

1 An emerald-cut sapphire (43.2 carats) and diamond ring. New York $170,500 (£95,251). 22.IV.82
2 An emerald (11.83 carats) and diamond ring by Cartier. New York $187,000 (£104,469). 13.X.81
   From the collection of Mrs Walter Buhl Ford II
3 A cushion-shaped ruby (8.67 carats) and diamond ring by Winston. New York $440,000 (£245,810). 13.X.81
4 A marquise-shaped fancy yellow diamond (40.7 carats) ring. New York $605,000 (£337,989). 22.IV.82
5 An emerald-cut fancy yellow diamond (12.05 carats) ring. New York $247,500 (£138,268). 14.X.81
6 An oval-cut ruby (7.14 carats) and diamond ring by Cartier. New York $132,000 (£73,743). 14.X.81
   From the collection of Mrs Walter Buhl Ford II
7 A circular-cut diamond (21.33 carats) ring. New York $352,000 (£196,648). 21.IV.82
8 An oval-cut ruby (approx 6.65 carats) and diamond ring. Hong Kong HK $275,000 (£26,699:$47,791). 23.XI.81

From left to right
An emerald bracelet by Cartier. $17,600 (£9,832)
An emerald and diamond clip by Cartier, the emerald weighing approximately 13.5 carats.
$60,500 (£33,799)
A pearl necklace by Chaumet. $126,500 (£70,670)
A pair of emerald and diamond pendent earrings by Cartier. $99,000 (£55,307)

The jewellery illustrated on this page was sold in New York on 9 June 1982

Above
A pair of pearl and diamond pendent earrings. SFr 37,400 (£10,447:$18,700)
Centre
An Art Deco emerald and diamond bracelet. SFr 46,200 (£12,905:$23,100)
Below
A pair of emerald and diamond pendent earrings. SFr 165,000 (£46,089:$82,499)

The jewellery illustrated on this page was sold in St Moritz on 20 February 1982

An emerald and diamond brooch by Van Cleef & Arpels, the emerald weighing approximately 13 carats and the diamonds approximately 15.5 carats. $33,000 (£18,436)
A diamond necklace with a detachable pendant, the pendent diamond weighing 8.18 carats. The necklace $36,300 (£20,279); the pendant $187,000 (£104,469)

The jewellery illustrated above was sold in New York on 10 June 1982

Opposite
A sapphire and diamond necklace which divides to form two separate necklaces
St Moritz SFr 550,000 (£153,631:$274,999). 20.II.82
From the collection of HSH Mathildis, Duchess of Arenberg de Callays

Antiquities and Asian art

An Egyptian bronze figure of Horus, Ptolemaic–
Early Roman period, *circa* 305–1 BC, height 28½in
(72.4cm)
London £24,200 ($43,318). 5.VII.82
From the collection of the late Dr A. F. Philips

A Mesopotamian bronze alloy figure of a bull, *circa* 2000–1500 BC, height 13⅝in (34.6cm)
New York $42,900(£23,966). 9.XII.81
From the collection of Professor and Mrs Robert N. Ganz Jr

A South Arabian alabaster head, *circa* first
century BC–first century AD, height 9½in (24.1cm)
London £18,700 ($33,473). 5.VII.82
From the collection of W. J. Merson

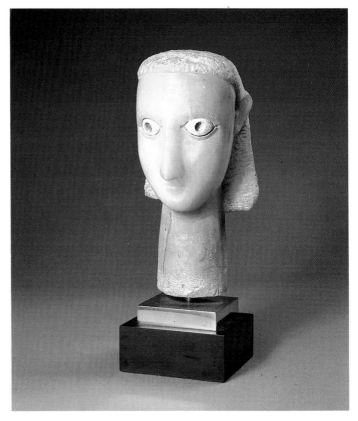

Below
An Attic red-figure cup by the Antiphon
Painter, *circa* 490–480 BC,
diameter 12¼in (31.1cm)
London £20,350 ($36,427). 14.XII.81

An Attic red-figure bell krater belonging to the group of Polygnotos, *circa* 450–440 BC, diameter $17\frac{7}{8}$in (45.4cm)
London £28,600 ($51,194). 5.VII.82

An Attic black-figure amphora belonging to the Botkin class, in a style related to the Phrynos Painter, second half sixth century BC, height $11\frac{1}{4}$in (28.5cm)
London £28,600($51,194). 5.VII.82

An Attic red-figure stamnos by the Achilles Painter, *circa* 450 BC, height 11⅝in (29.5cm)
London £28,600 ($51,194). 5.VII.82

A Roman bronze head of a man, *circa* first–second century AD, height of head $12\frac{1}{8}$in (30.8cm)
London £121,000($216,590). 14.XII.81

A Greco-Roman marble figure of Pan, *circa* second half first century AD, height 26⅝in (67.6cm)
New York $48,400 (£27,039). 20.V.82

A Sinhalese polychrome wood mask of the chief Sanni demon (Maha-Kola
Sanni Yaka), height 50¾in (128.9cm)
London £3,960 ($7,088). 30.III.82

A Tibetan bronze figure of a *Yi-dam*, possibly Vajrakila, sixteenth century, height 22¼in (56.5cm)
New York $30,800 (£17,207). 18.XII.81

Primitive art

A north-eastern Plains quilled hide shirt with a wool beaded collar, late eighteenth–early nineteenth century, length 33½in (85.1cm)
New York $41,250(£23,045). 24.IV.82
From the collection of the Messiter family

This shirt was part of a collection of American Indian art made by the English hunter and traveller Charles Alston Messiter (1841–1920). He described his first three visits to North America in his book *Sport and Adventures amongst the North American Indians* (1890)

One of a pair of Mayan moulded pottery cache vessels, Early Classic period, height 19in (48.2cm)
New York $137,500 (£76,816). 5.XII.81

Navajo textiles

Mark Winter

The ability of Navajo women to weave textiles that are both beautiful and marketable has been recognized by all who have come into contact with them since the tribe first adapted to the loom over 300 years ago. These textiles are held in as much esteem by collectors today as they were by this nomadic tribe themselves, who initially relied on the finely designed and woven blankets for protection against the harsh elements of south-western North America.

The Navajo are of the Athabaskan linguistic group and migrated from the North, apparently seeking a warmer climate. By 1400, they had settled north of the stone and adobe fortress villages of the Pueblo Indians of the Upper Rio Grande Valley, in what is now New Mexico, and to the west, in what is now Arizona. Trade appears to have been established between the Pueblo and the Navajo prior to the arrival of the Spanish in 1540.

Led by Coronado, the Spanish came up the Rio Grande Valley searching for the Seven Cities of Gold. In 1598, their conquest of the Pueblo Indians resulted in the establishment of settlements under a colonial government. The Navajo witnessed the plight of the Pueblo and kept their distance: historical records show that while they traded with the Spanish, they also raided their northern settlements. Over the next 250 years, despite the struggle for control of the Southwest between the Pueblo Indians, the Spanish, the Mexicans and United States troops, the Navajo developed and maintained an independent culture.

It was during this period, probably *circa* 1600–50, that the Navajo started turning cotton cloth-weaving on the primitive upright loom, learned from the Pueblo people, into a highly sophisticated textile art. They produced various types of finely woven textiles, including shirts, dresses and wearing blankets, using wool from stolen Spanish Churro sheep as their primary material. The primitive upright loom has continued to this day to be the only type of loom used by the Navajo weavers.

In 1795, the Spanish Governor of New Mexico, Fernando de Chacón admitted that the rebel Navajo, 'work their wool with more delicacy and taste than the Spaniards'. Pedro Piño in his *Expedición a Nuevo Mexico* (1812), described Navajo textiles as, 'woollen fabrics that are the most valuable goods in our province as well as Sonora and Chihuahua'. Even as far north as the Great Plains, traders recorded that during the 1840s, the Indians were willing to trade at least ten good buffalo robes for a single Navajo blanket. In 1849, Lieutenant James H. Simpson of the United States army commented on the Navajo, who 'seemed so poor', yet 'capable of making probably the best blankets in the world'.

Fig 1
A Navajo child's blanket in ravelled red Bayeta, three-ply Saxony and handspun yarn,
Classic period, *circa* 1865–75, 2ft 6in by 3ft 8¼in (76.2cm by 112.4cm)
New York $8,250 (£4,609). 24.IV.82

When the United States government took possession of much of the south-western territory in the 1850s, the bold roving nature of the Navajo became such a threat to the white settlers that the army was despatched in 1861 under Kit Carson to solve the 'Navajo problem'. By 1863, the Navajo had been herded off their lands and moved to an encampment near Fort Sumner, called Bosque Redondo, in southern New Mexico. They remained there for five years and were finally returned to what was then, and is still, considered their homeland, the present Navajo reservation. This site consists of over sixteen million acres and is the largest reservation in the United States.

Thus began a change in lifestyle which drastically affected the textiles of this victimized race. The army had destroyed Navajo herds and burned most of their blankets in an attempt to break the native spirit. At Bosque Redondo, they were

Fig 2
A Navajo chief's blanket in red and green ravelled Bayeta, and brown, white and indigo-blue-dyed handspun yarn, Classic period, *circa* 1860–70, 4ft 8$\frac{1}{2}$in by 5ft 10$\frac{1}{2}$in (143.5cm by 179cm)
New York $31,900(£17,821). 23.X.81

This blanket illustrates the second phase of textile decoration within the Classic period, when red designs were incorporated into the simple banded blanket, characteristic of the first phase. These designs ultimately developed into the large terraced diamonds which distinguish the third phase

Fig 3
A Navajo chief's blanket in single-ply commercial yarn, Transitional period, *circa* 1890–1900,
5ft 4½in by 6ft 6¼in (163.9cm by 198.8cm)
New York $8,800 (£4,916). 23.X.81

This pattern is typical of the third phase of design within the Classic period, although the blanket is of
a slightly later date. It is rare in being entirely woven from commercial yarn

issued with Merino sheep, which provided food, but the wool proved to be not as adaptable to south-western handspinning. Commercial yarn from Germantown, Pennsylvania, was issued in large quantities and became a preferred material. World-wide discoveries also affected the blankets produced on the Navajo looms. Chemical dyes were discovered in Europe in 1857 and became available almost immediately: after about 1875 they were the dyes predominantly used. The perfection of the mechanical loom for cloth production led to the opening of woollen mills producing good, inexpensive blankets, which were distributed to the tribe. The adaptation of the Navajo mode of dress to the style of the white man completed a change of emphasis in the use of their textiles. Navajo weavers remained active but woven goods became popular trade items, particularly as rugs.

Navajo weaving can be divided into three distinct periods, using material and design as the primary criteria: although traditional forms were copied at all times. The earliest period, until about 1875, is considered the 'Classic period' (Figs 1–2). The material used was handspun Churro wool in natural brown and white, or dyed indigo-blue. The Navajo were fascinated by red, which was all around them in the landscape, but lacking a good natural dye, they re-used ravelled threads from 'Bayeta', a Navajo term for commercial red tradecloths. A small amount of three-ply imported Saxony yarn was also used (Fig 1). Designs were bold variations on striped and terraced half-diamond schemes positioned symmetrically on the blanket to accent the body, as the garment was worn. These textiles are the most valuable to current collectors (see *Art at Auction 1980–81*, p 452).

After 1875, pieces exploded with colour as the European dyes were exploited, and new materials were introduced (Fig 3), predominantly the Germantown yarn. It was the first time that the Navajo weaver had had such a wide palette with which to work. The 'Transitional period', as it is known, lasted until about 1900, when the transition from blankets to rugs was complete. Angular serrated designs, derived from Spanish colonial weaving, dominated these so-called 'eye-dazzler' textiles (Fig 4). Transitional-period weavings are not yet as highly sought after as Classic examples, but the greater availability of Transitional items has made for a very active market.

Gaudy synthetic dyes did not suit late Victorian taste, so traders around 1900 encouraged the Navajo to return to native materials to produce a textile to compete with Oriental rugs. Each trader in his own region of the reservation encouraged weavers to develop the complex multi-bordered designs he felt would be most marketable. These rugs, from twenty-five to seventy-five years old, are grouped under the heading of 'Regional styles', and have received much attention in the last few years. They contain excellent graphic designs, are very durable and warm, have an attractive hand-made quality and are reasonably priced considering the expert workmanship involved.

It is only in recent times that Navajo weavers have produced textiles as well woven as Classic-period pieces. The quality has risen to suit the taste of more discerning buyers and, although the number of weavers capable of this work is small, modern weavers are receiving much attention for their achievements. Recently too, museums, dealers and collectors have sponsored many exhibitions throughout the world,

Fig 4
A Navajo 'eye-dazzler' blanket in Germantown yarn, Transitional period, *circa* 1880–90,
4ft 11½in by 7ft 4in (151.2cm by 223.5cm)
New York $4,950(£2,765). 24.IV.82

creating an upsurge of interest in Navajo textiles. Fortunately, the weavers were prolific and a surprising number of well-preserved examples survive. Some collectors are now also taking an interest in more obscure areas of Navajo and south-western textiles. For example, Spanish colonial Saltillo serapes from northern Mexico are particularly popular.

In the drama of the Southwest, the function of Navajo textiles has changed with the changing rôle of the people themselves. However, it was and still is the Navajo women who control the warp and weft. The patterns of the blankets reflect and transcend the rugged but picturesque landscape, meeting the demands of its harshness with brave, bold and beautiful adornment.

A Tlingit wood clan hat, Alaska, nineteenth century, diameter $14\frac{1}{2}$in (36.8cm)
New York $66,000 (£36,872). 23.X.81

A Vili wood ceremonial bell, Zaire,
height 7$\frac{1}{4}$in (18.4cm)
London £14,300 ($25,597). 30.XI.81

An eastern Woodlands wood bowl, seventeenth century, width 6$\frac{1}{4}$in (15.8cm)
New York $110,000 (£61,453). 24.IV.82

A Fang wood male reliquary figure, Okak tribe, Equatorial Guinea, height 14$\frac{1}{4}$in (36.2cm)
London £41,800 ($74,822). 6.VII.82

An Hawaiian wood and sharks' teeth scarifying weapon (*palau papanihomano*), inscribed *HAWAII IS. (COOK)*, length 15¾in (40cm)
London £27,500 ($49,225). 6.VII.82

This weapon was collected on Captain Cook's third voyage to Hawaii in 1778–79

Islamic textiles and works of art

A Turkman Yomut *asmalik*, mid nineteenth century, 2ft 9in by 4ft 5in (84cm by 134.5cm)
New York $48,400 (£27,039). 30.X.81

A Bordjalou Kazak rug, mid nineteenth century, 7ft by 5ft 3in (213.5cm by 160cm)
New York $46,750(£26,117). 31.X.81

An Heriz silk rug, nineteenth century, 6ft 3½in by 4ft 9in (192cm by 145cm)
Geneva SFr 52,800 (£14,749 : $26,401). 13.XI.81

An Heriz silk pictorial carpet, depicting the court of Alexander and the punishment of
Jalinous, nineteenth century, 12ft 11½in by 9ft 2½in (395cm by 281cm)
Geneva SFr 143,000 (£39,944 : $71,500). 7.V.82

A Bessarabian carpet, eighteenth century, 11ft 7in by 8ft 11in (353cm by 272cm)
London £10,120 ($18,115). 28.IV.82

Opposite
A north-western Persian animal and tree carpet, eighteenth century,
14ft 5in by 8ft 5in (439.5cm by 256.5cm)
London £8,250 ($14,768). 14.X.81

An Iranian facet-cut glass bottle, ninth–tenth century, height 6½in (16.5cm)
London £13,750 ($24,613). 26.IV.82
From the collection of Madame Lin

This bottle is reputed to have been recovered from the tomb of a Tang Dynasty aristocrat near Xian, China, in 1948

An Isnik 'Damascus' pottery dish, mid sixteenth century, diameter 15in (38.1cm)
London £12,650 ($22,644). 26.IV.82

A Syrian painted wood room in the 'Turkish Rococo' style, comprising three walls and a ceiling, and
the ceiling of an adjacent room, dated AH 1205 (1790–91 AD), the room 15ft 3in by 10ft 4in
(465cm by 315cm), height 11ft 10in (360cm); the ceiling 15ft 3in by 14ft 5¼in (465cm by 440cm)
London £28,600 ($51,194). 26.IV.82

An Indo-Persian dagger with gold-mounted and jewelled jade hilt, late eighteenth century,
length 17$\frac{1}{4}$in (43.8cm)
London £3,740($6,695). 17.XI.81

A Mughal jade ewer and cover, seventeenth–eighteenth century, height 10¼in (26cm)
London £19,800 ($35,442). 8.VI.82

Chinese ceramics, works of art and paintings

A northern celadon tripod censer, Northern Song Dynasty, diameter $8\frac{7}{8}$in (22.6cm)
London £115,500 ($206,745). 15.XII.81

A *yingqing* figure of Buddha, Yuan Dynasty, height $20\frac{7}{8}$in (53cm)
Hong Kong HK $1,155,000(£112,136:$200,723). 24.XI.81

Above
A Ming blue and white brush-rest, six character mark and period of Zhengde, width 8⅝in (21.9cm)
New York $26,400 (£14,749). 6.XI.81
Below
A Ming blue and white brush-handle, six character mark and period of Xuande, length 5⅝in (14.2cm)
New York $35,200 (£19,665). 6.XI.81
From the collection of the late John A. Foster

A Ming blue and white rose-water sprinkler, Yongle period, height $8\frac{1}{8}$in (20.6cm)
Hong Kong HK \$1,320,000 (£128,155:\$229,397). 18.V.82
From the collection of Frederick Knight

A Ming underglaze-red decorated dish, Hongwu period, diameter 18⅛in (46cm)
Hong Kong HK $2,530,000(£245,631:$439,679). 24.XI.81

A Ming blue and white potiche (*guan*), six character mark and period of Jiajing, diameter 12⅝in (32cm)
Hong Kong HK $1,265,000 (£122,816:$219,841). 24.XI.81

A Ming blue and white leys jar (*zhadou*), four character mark and period of Zhengde,
diameter 5⅞in (14.9cm)
Hong Kong HK $550,000(£53,398:$95,582). 18.V.82
From the collection of Frederick Knight

A Ming blue and white bowl, Yongle period, diameter 7¾in (19.6cm)
Hong Kong HK $1,100,000(£106,796:$191,165). 18.V.82
From the collection of Frederick Knight

A Ming blue and white moon flask (*bianhu*), Yongle period, height 9¾in (24.7cm)
Hong Kong HK $990,000 (£96,117:$172,049). 18.V.82

A Ming blue and white dragon dish, six character mark and period of Chenghua,
diameter 12$\frac{1}{8}$in (30.9cm)
Hong Kong HK $3,190,000 (£309,709:$554,379). 24.XI.81

A yellow-ground vase, seal mark and period of Qianlong,
height 22⅝in (57.5cm)
Hong Kong HK $572,000 (£55,534:$99,406). 19.V.82

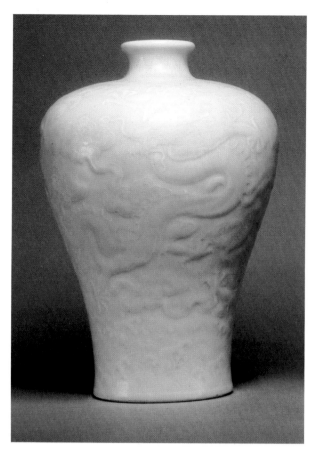

A carved and moulded celadon vase (*meiping*), seal mark and period of Qianlong, height 13in (33cm) New York $60,500(£33,799). 4.VI.82

A moulded celadon flask, seal mark and period of Yongzheng, height 9in (22.8cm) New York $57,200(£31,955). 4.VI.82

Opposite
A peach-bloom chrysanthemum vase, six character mark and period of Kangxi, height 8½in (21.5cm)
Hong Kong HK $1,100,000(£106,796:$191,165). 25.XI.81

A pair of Chinese export figures of eagles, Qianlong period, height of each $22\frac{7}{8}$ in (58cm)
Monte Carlo FF 444,000 (£40,511:$72,515). 9.II.82

Opposite
A Chinese export dinner service with the arms of Don Antonio José de Castro, Bishop of Oporto,
Jiaqing period
Monte Carlo FF 2,053,500 (£187,363:$335,380). 9.II.82

An archaic bronze axe-head, early Western Zhou Dynasty, height 7in (17.7cm)
London £74,800 ($133,892). 15.XII.81

Opposite
A *huang huali* low table, sixteenth century, width 36¼in (92.1cm)
New York $33,000 (£18,436). 7.XI.81

A Ming cinnabar lacquer box
and cover, six character mark
and period of Yongle,
diameter 5¾in (14.7cm)
Hong Kong HK $396,000
(£38,447:$68,820). 18.V.82
From the collection of
Frederick Knight

A polychrome wood figure of Guanyin, twelfth century, height 86in (218.5cm)
New York $187,000(£104,469). 6.XI.81
From the collection of the late Anne Burnett Tandy

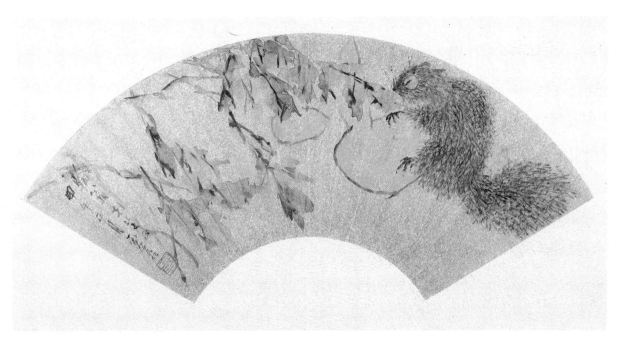

XU GU
Squirrel and gourd
Fan painting, ink and colour on gold-flecked paper, signed, inscribed and dated 1894,
$7\frac{3}{8}$in by $21\frac{1}{4}$in (18.8cm by 54cm)
New York $8,250(£4,609). 5.XI.81
From the collection of the late Chan Yee Pong

ZHANG DAQIAN
Giant lotus
A set of six hanging scrolls, ink and colour on paper, signed and with four seals of the artist, inscribed
and dated 1960–61, $140\frac{1}{4}$in by 315in (356.2cm by 800cm)
New York $77,000(£43,017). 4.VI.82

Chinese snuff bottles –
the Bob C. Stevens Collection

Robert Kleiner

Until recently, Chinese snuff bottles were taken seriously by few of those interested in the more profound areas of Chinese art and achievement. Nevertheless, snuff bottles are a microcosm of Chinese works of art of the eighteenth and nineteenth centuries, and they are of importance in the study of all the achievements of that period because of their rôle in the court life of the time. Usually no more than two or three inches high, their small size was an ideal medium within which artists and craftsmen could excel to the utmost. The best examples of Chinese enamel work, overlay-glass and miniature hardstone carving are to be found in the realm of the snuff bottle. The collection of the late Bob C. Stevens was one of the finest, containing examples covering the complete range in quality, date and materials. It therefore provides an ideal field for the study of their history and development.

Tobacco was probably introduced into China during the Wanli (1573–1619) or Tianqi (1621–27) period.[1] Smoking was found to be unacceptable and soon banned, but snuff was considered medicinal. The Ruzhen, or Manchu Tartars from the North particularly favoured snuff. They conquered China in 1644, assuming the dynastic title of Qing and it is to this invading race that the earliest snuff bottles can be attributed: a group of brass bottles bear dates between 1644 and 1653, together with the reign name of the first Qing emperor, Shunzhi. These bottles are of sturdy manufacture, well suited to the needs of a warrior race (Fig 1). The traditional attributes of the snuff bottle are already established: a small rounded shape to fit into a pouch, a flat bottom for resting on a table and a stopper fitted with a cork and an ivory spoon.

The major impetus to the development of the snuff bottle was given by the succeeding emperor who took the reign title of Kangxi (1662–1722). He was a keen snuff taker, as is revealed by a number of sources. An examination of a list of gifts sent to the emperor in 1684, shows that snuff was the only item he retained.[2]

---

[1] Zhang Yaolun 'Chi'ing-tai yen-tsu wen-chien-lu', *Shuowen Monthly*, Zhuan II, no 2. The author is grateful for most of the references in this article to Gerard C. C. Tsang 'Chinese Views on Snuff', in the exhibition catalogue, *Chinese Snuff Bottles* (Hong Kong Museum of Art, 1977), and to H. M. Moss and Gerard C. C. Tsang, Foreword to the exhibition catalogue, *Snuff Bottles of the Ch'ing Dynasty* (Hong Kong Museum of Art, 1978)

[2] Verbiest, F. *Hsi-chao ting-an* (Taiwan, nd)

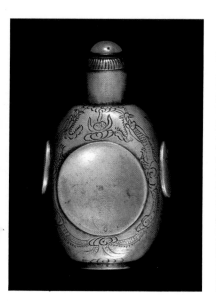

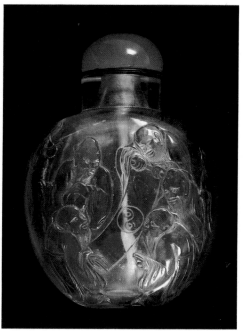

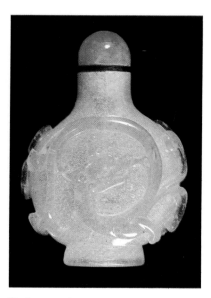

Fig 1
A brass snuff bottle, mark and period
of Shunzhi, inscribed and dated 1646
Honolulu $6,600 (£3,687). 7. XI.81
From the collection of the late
Bob C. Stevens

Fig 2
A Peking glass snuff bottle, inscribed,
1750–1850
Honolulu $18,700 (£10,447). 7.XI.81
From the collection of the late Bob C. Stevens

Fig 3
An overlay-glass snuff bottle,
mid eighteenth century
Honolulu $1,430 (£799). 7.XI.81
From the collection of the late
Bob C. Stevens

The emperor established workshops within the palace in Peking during the 1680s for the manufacture of a wide variety of small items for court use, in particular, glass and enamels. The scholar, Wang Shizhen, writing in 1705, states: 'The country of Luzon [the Philippines] produces a leaf for smoking called "tobacco". When it arrives at the capital it is made into snuff . . . Glass bottles of every shape are made to contain it. The colours are red, purple, yellow, white, black and green; the white is like crystal and the red is like fire. Things of great delight. There is an ivory spoon which is returned to the flask after snuffing. They are all manufactured within the palace. Imitations are made by the common people but they never attain to the standard of the original.'[3] The Stevens Collection was rich in glass bottles, many of which can be attributed to the eighteenth century on grounds of quality, style and comparison with dated examples, incised with the four character mark of the Qianlong emperor (1736–95). Fine examples continued to be made into the nineteenth century (Fig 2).

A further development in the manufacture of glass bottles at this time was the technique of carving in cameo style, applying different colours of overlay. Red and blue were the earliest colours, but as the craftsmen achieved mastery the range of colours and the subject matter of the designs increased. The powerful coiled *chilong* in pale lime yellow is typical of the mid eighteenth century (Fig 3).

[3] Wang Shizen *Xianci Biji* (Shanghai, nd), Zhuan VII

Fig 4
An enamelled glass snuff bottle, Peking
palace workshops, four character mark
and period of Qianlong
Honolulu $18,150 (£10,140). 7.XI.81
From the collection of the late
Bob C. Stevens

Fig 5
An enamelled glass snuff bottle, Peking
palace workshops, four character mark
and period of Qianlong
New York $28,050 (£15,670). 25.VI.82
From the collection of the late
Bob C. Stevens

Fig 6
An enamelled glass snuff bottle
by Ye Pengqi, early twentieth
century
New York $9,625 (£5,377).
25.VI.82
From the collection of the late
Bob C. Stevens

The most highly prized of all snuff bottles, however, were those enamelled on copper or glass. Father Matteo Ripa, writing in 1716, states: 'His Majesty having become fascinated by our European enamel and by the new method of enamel painting, tried by every possible means to introduce the latter into his imperial workshops which he had set up for this purpose within the palace.'[4] Several years were to pass before the Chinese fully mastered the art of enamelling and the majority of the finest enamelled examples date from the Qianlong period. Scenes depicting Europeans and subjects in Chinese taste were both popular, the finest and rarest of the group being enamelled on a glass body (Figs 4–5). These bottles were extremely difficult to produce successfully, due to the low melting point of the body during firing, as opposed to the high fusion point of the enamel decoration. The great majority of the known examples of this type, some forty or so, are in the National Palace Museum in Taiwan,[5] but the Stevens Collection possessed three.

One example (Fig 5) is of outstanding interest, because it may be compared with another group of enamelled glass bottles of the highest quality, manufactured during

[4] *Memoirs of Father Ripa during Thirteen Years Residence at the Court of Peking* selected and translated from the Italian by F. Prandix (London, 1844)
[5] Lin Sheng Zhang 'Snuff Bottles in the National Palace Museum, Taiwan', *Journal of the International Chinese Snuff Bottle Society*, March 1979

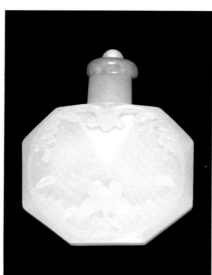

Fig 7
A Suzhou chalcedony snuff bottle,
1750–1850
Honolulu $17,050(£9,525). 7.XI.81
From the collection of the late
Bob C. Stevens

Fig 8
A jade snuff bottle, Peking palace
workshops, eighteenth century
Honolulu $21,450(£11,983). 7.XI.81
From the collection of the late
Bob C. Stevens

Fig 9
A Yixing snuff bottle, 1800–50
Honolulu $27,500(£15,363).
7.XI.81
From the collection of the late
Bob C. Stevens

the early years of this century by a family of skilled artists, the Ye, better known as painters of the interiors of snuff bottles.[6] This work was initiated by Ye Zhongsan and carried on by one of his sons, Ye Pengqi. They used to visit the Peking Museum after the Republic was established in 1912, and make copies of the imperial glass bottles on display. One of the best examples of this group is in the Stevens Collection (Fig 6), and this is clearly inspired by the original referred to above. A comparison of the two is therefore of great value in establishing the differences of treatment. The leaves and flowers on the original are much freer than those on the copy, which has the flowers outlined in red. The elaborate collar on the original is slightly better controlled. The shapes are different, but early cylindrical bottles are known. Perhaps the most significant difference lies in the reign mark on the base. The original has the four character Qianlong mark incised and filled in with blue enamel, whereas the copy merely has the mark enamelled on top of the surface. This is a detail which the Ye family, being unable to handle the originals, could not have seen.

Whilst the greatest interest during this period centred on glass and enamelled bottles, a wide variety of other materials was used. Jade (Fig 8) and chalcedony (Fig 7) were particularly favoured and fine examples were made both in the palace work-

[6] Moss, H. M. *By Imperial Command* (Hong Kong, 1976), pp 65–67

Fig 10
An interior-painted glass
snuff bottle by Zhou Leyuan,
signed and inscribed
New York $4,675 (£2,612).
26.III.82
From the collection of the
late Bob C. Stevens

Fig 11
An interior-painted glass
snuff bottle by Ding
Erzhong, signed and
dated 1896
New York $2,200 (£1,229).
26.III.82
From the collection of the
late Bob C. Stevens

Fig 12
An interior-painted glass
snuff bottle by Ye Zhongsan
the Elder, signed and dated
1902
New York $4,180 (£2,335).
26.III.82
From the collection of the
late Bob C. Stevens

Fig 13
An interior-painted glass
snuff bottle by
Ma Shaoxuan, signed,
inscribed and dated 1924
New York $4,950 (£2,765).
25.VI.82
From the collection of the
late Bob C. Stevens

Fig 14
An interior-painted rock-
crystal snuff bottle with
a portrait of Duanfang,
Governor of Sichuan
province, by Ma Shaoxuan,
signed, inscribed and dated
1907
New York $10,450 (£5,838).
25.VI.82
From the collection of the
late Bob C. Stevens

Fig 15
An interior-painted rock-
crystal portrait snuff bottle
by Ma Shaoxuan, signed,
inscribed and dated 1912
New York $22,000 (£12,291).
26.III.82
From the collection of the
late Bob C. Stevens

Fig 16
An interior-painted glass
snuff bottle with a portrait
of the actor Tan Xinpei by
Ma Shaoxuan, signed and
inscribed
New York $3,300 (£1.844).
26.III.82
From the collection of the
late Bob C. Stevens

Fig 17
An interior-painted glass
snuff bottle with a portrait
of the actor Tan Xinpei by
Ciyici, signed and dated
1901
New York $6,325 (£3,534).
26.III.82
From the collection of the
late Bob C. Stevens

shops and in provincial centres such as Suzhou, which was well known for its hardstone carving.[7] The chalcedony bottle illustrated above, is a quintessential example of this school, in which brilliant use is made of any natural inclusions in the stone to create scenes, usually recessed and framed by serrated rock-work.

Imperial patronage contributed greatly to the popularity of the snuff bottle and, as the nineteenth century approached, the habit of snuff taking began to filter down the social scale. Demand increased and quality declined, but some centres such as Yixing, in Jiangsu province, famous for its pottery wares, maintained a certain elegance, as the Stevens example with its delicate slip design demonstrates (Fig 9). The range of materials increased to include moulded gourds, coral, aquamarine, topaz and bamboo, among others.

Artistic decline continued as the nineteenth century proceeded, and there was little innovation in Chinese art after the reign of the Daoguang emperor (1821–50). One of the few interesting new art forms, however, was that of painting on the interior of glass or rock-crystal snuff bottles, so that the scene was visible through the transparent walls. Bamboo pens sharply curved at the tip were inserted through the narrow opening to paint on the inside surface, which was roughened to receive the pigment. This technique was developed by an artist working under the name of Ganhuan, and examples of his work exist dated between 1816 and 1865.

The true master of the school was Zhou Leyuan who painted in a classical Chinese style with consummate skill,[8] as may be seen from an ink composition of bamboos (Fig 10). This artist was active between 1882 and 1893, and inspired a host of others, several of whom became highly skilled and sought after in their own right. Ding Erzhong, a scholar and seal carver, copied Song paintings (Fig 11), and examples of his work are difficult to find. Ye Zhongsan, referred to above, painted in a more European style (Fig 12), as did Ma Shaoxuan (Fig 13). The portrait bottles by Ma Shaoxuan are of great technical interest and merit. They depict political figures and dignitaries of the last years of the Qing Dynasty: the Governor of Sichuan province, Duanfang (Fig 14), was responsible for the evacuation of the Empress Dowager Cixi from Peking in 1900, during the Boxer uprising.[9] The subject of another fine bottle has not yet been identified (Fig 15). The Stevens Collection contained two portrait bottles of the great Qing actor, Tan Xinpei, in the rôle of General Huang Zhong; one by Ma Shaoxuan (Fig 16), and one by another rare and highly regarded artist, Ciyici (Fig 17). It is of interest to compare the photographic style of the former with the more impressionistic style of the latter.

Throughout Chinese history, imperial patronage has played a significant part in inspiring and encouraging the development of the arts. This patronage was fully bestowed upon snuff bottles under the Qing Dynasty, resulting in a high level of achievement. A study of snuff bottles therefore adds greatly to our knowledge of the arts of the Qing.

---

[7] Moss, H. M. 'Group C: The Soochow School', *Chinese Snuff Bottles of the Quartz or Silica Group* (London, 1971)

[8] Moss, H. M. 'How to Buy Interior-painted Snuff Bottles: 3 Chou Lo-yuan', in *Chinese Snuff Bottles, no 4* (Warwick, 1966)

[9] Curtiss, E. B. *Reflected Glory in a Snuff Bottle* (New York, 1980), p33

A jade jar and cover, Qianlong period, height $8\frac{1}{4}$in (21cm)
London £30,800 ($55,132). 8.VI.82

An Imperial jade brush-pot, Kangxi period, diameter of brush-pot $8\frac{7}{8}$in (22.5cm)
London £53,900($96,481). 8.VI.82

Japanese paintings, prints, works of art and ceramics

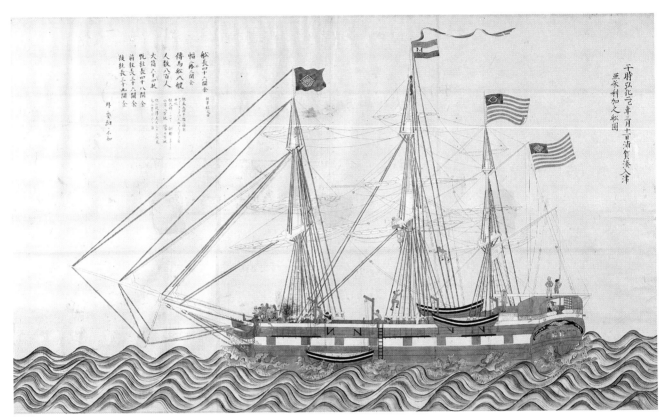

JAPANESE SCHOOL
The American whale ship 'Manhattan' in Japanese waters
Watercolour, dated 1845, 27in by 44in (68.6cm by 111.8cm)
New York $82,500 (£46,089). 11.XII.81
From the collection of Barbara Johnson

The *Manhattan* arrived off Tokyo in March 1845 to repatriate thirteen rescued Japanese seamen, in spite of Japan's policy of excluding foreign vessels. Great interest was shown in the ship and it departed ceremoniously a month later, although the captain was forbidden ever to return to Japan

EISHOSAI CHOKI
A beauty with an umbrella under falling snow
Oban, 13¾in by 8⅞in (35cm by 22.5cm)
London £16,500 ($29,535). 28.X.81

A *shakudo nanako tsuba* by
Ishiguro Masatsune, signed,
diameter 3in (7.6cm)
London £5,720 ($10,239).
17.III.82

A *sentoku* and *shibuichi tsuba*
by Masayoshi, signed,
diameter $2\frac{7}{8}$in (7.3cm)
London £2,640 ($4,726).
27.X.81

A soft-metal *tsuba* by Riuso
Hogen, signed and dated 1854,
diameter $2\frac{7}{8}$in (7.3cm)
London £3,300 ($5,907).
23.VI.82

A *shibuichi tsuba, kozuka* and *fuchi-kashira* by Rinsendo Mitsumasa, each signed, diameter of
tsuba $2\frac{5}{8}$in (6.5cm)
London £2,750 ($4,923). 27.X.81
From the collection of the late Lt Col H.A.W. Backhoff, MM

Left
A *tachi* blade by Kanesada (*shu-mei* attribution), with mounts by Masatoshi, signed, length of blade 27⅛in (68.9cm)
London £15,400 ($27,566). 23.VI.82
From the collection of the late Field Marshal Sir Francis Festing, GCB, KBE, DSO

Right
An *aikuchi* blade by Yamoto Masanori (second generation), with mounts ascribed to Ishiguro Masayoshi, length of blade 11¾in (29.8cm)
London £11,000 ($19,690). 17.III.82

An ivory study of a *kirin* by
Masanao, signed, Kyoto,
circa 1781
New York $26,400 (£14,749).
8.XII.81

A wood study of a monkey by
Kano Tomokazu, signed, Gifu,
nineteenth century
New York $7,700 (£4,302).
17.IX.81
From the collection of the late
Mary Louise O'Brien

An ivory study of a cat
with a rat by Tomotada,
signed, Kyoto, late
eighteenth century
London £19,690 ($35,245).
24.VI.82

An ivory figure of a Chinaman,
eighteenth century
London £11,000 ($19,690).
26.X.81

A lacquer *inro* by Koma Ankyo
(Yasutada), signed, nineteenth
century
London £2,420 ($4,332). 17.III.82

An ivory figure of a Chinese
merchant, late eighteenth
century
London £3,850 ($6,892). 26.X.81

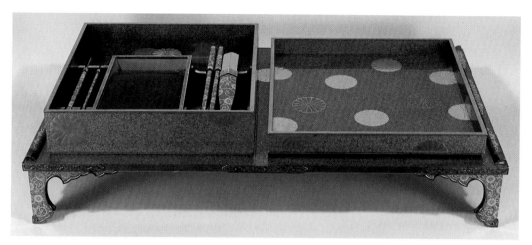

A *suzuribako* with matching table, late Edo–Meiji period, width of table 23⅜in (59.2cm)
London £8,250($14,768). 26.X.81

A pair of Shibayama vases by Koryu, signed, late nineteenth century, height of each 9⅞in (25cm)
London £5,500($9,845). 29.X.81

A *cloisonné* vase by Ando Jubei, signed, *circa* 1900, height 13¾in (35cm)
London £21,450 ($38,396). 11.III.82

A bronze group of Tametomo and two *oni* by Miyao, signed, late nineteenth century, height 29⅞in (76cm)
London £16,500 ($29,535). 29.X.81

A pair of Kakiemon tigers, late seventeenth century, height of each $9\frac{7}{8}$in (25.2cm);
$9\frac{1}{2}$in (24.3cm)
London £24,200 ($43,318). 26.X.81
From the collection of Sally Lloyd-Williams

Two from a set of five Nabeshima underglaze-blue and enamel dishes, late seventeenth–early
eighteenth century, diameter of each 8in (20.3cm)
New York $198,000 (£110,615). 8.VI.82
From the collection of Jeffery Story and Walter Cook

A Kakiemon double-gourd bottle, late seventeenth century, height 16in (40.6cm)
New York $72,600 (£40,559). 8.VI.82

Postage stamps

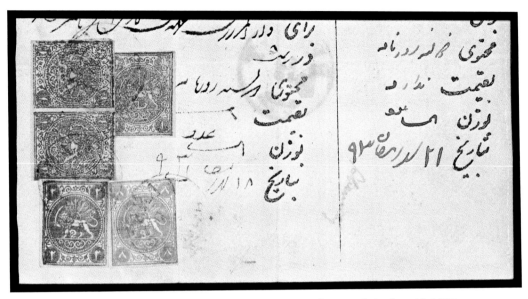

PERSIA, 1876 way bill, bearing 1876 1 kran carmine, horizontal pair and single, with 1875
2 shahi and 8 shahi and tied by Teheran cancellations
London £3,960($7,088). 6.XI.81

This way bill covered two parcels of newspapers sent to the Governor of Guilan at Rescht

LABUAN, double-ring circular date-stamp, struck in black on 1864 cover from England
London £1,760($3,150). 31.III.82

AUSTRALIA, 1912 4d Blamire
Young 'Kangaroo' essay
in pale orange
London £605 ($1,083).
18.IX.81

From the collection
of the late
James B. Williamson, FRPSL

GREAT BRITAIN, 1840 1d black, plate 5, unused strip of three
lettered JA–JC
Johannesburg R 11,000 (£5,699:$10,201). 22.IV.82

UNITED STATES OF
AMERICA, 1851–56
5¢ red-brown,
type I
New York $2,640
(£1,475). 9.II.82

FRANCE, 1870 entire letter, bearing 1870–71 20c
blue, flown out of the besieged city of Paris by
balloon ('ballon monté')
London £187 ($335). 30.III.82

UNITED STATES OF
AMERICA, 1880
2¢ scarlet-vermilion,
American Bank Note
Co Special Printing
New York $12,650
(£7,067). 9.II.82

FRANCE, 1870 Bordeaux 2c,
Report I, impression fine 'de
Tours', block of four
London £2,640 ($4,726).
30.III.82

GIBRALTAR, 1981 Royal Wedding £1, finished impression
incorporating alternative portraits, signed by the designer
A. G. Ryman, MBE
London £330 ($591). 16.XII.81

Collectors' sales and American folk art

A French prisoner-of-war-work bone and horn model of a sixty-gun second-rate ship of the line,
circa 1795, length 52in (132.1cm)
Chester £30,800 ($55,132). 24.VI.82
From the collection of the Earl of Sandwich 1943 Settlement

An American gilt-copper weathervane of the Statue of Liberty by the J. L. Mott Iron Works, New York
and Chicago, late nineteenth century, height 57in (144.8cm)
New York $82,500 (£46,089). 29.IV.82
From the collection of the late Thomas G. Rizzo

A French singing-bird automaton by Bontems,
circa 1880, height 21½in (54.5cm)
London £5,500 ($9,845). 10.II.82

Left
A German 24½-in 'Mikado' Polyphon disc
musical box on a disc cabinet, *circa* 1900,
height 86in (218.4cm)
London £5,280 ($9,451). 16.VII.82

A French character doll by Emile Jumeau, the bisque head impressed *Deposé Tête Jumeau Bte. 10 D.G.*, dated *1889*, height 22in (55.8cm) London £6,600 ($11,814). 10.II.82

A German tinplate gauge 'I' clockwork armoured train by Marklin, *circa* 1902 London £9,900 ($17,721). 13.V.82

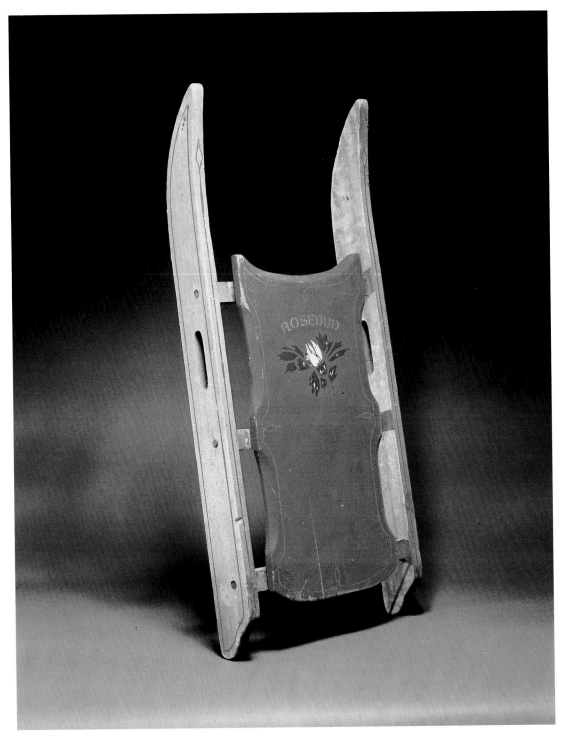

A wood sledge stamped ROSEBUD, used in the film *Citizen Kane*, released 1941, length 34in (86.4cm)
New York $60,500 (£33,799). 9.VI.82

In the opening scene of the film, 'rosebud' is the final word spoken by the dying publishing magnate
Kane, and the plot unfolds as a journalist tries to discover its meaning

A twelve-string Harptone guitar used by George Harrison of *The Beatles*, with
an authenticating letter, length 46in (116.8cm)
London £3,300 ($5,907). 22.XII.81

A detail from a celluloid of Mickey Mouse as the sorcerer's apprentice, from the film *Fantasia* by
Walt Disney, released 1940, $12\frac{1}{2}$in by $9\frac{3}{4}$in (31.7cm by 24.7cm)
New York $3,300 (£1,844). 10.XII.81

Scrimshaw from the Barbara Johnson Collection

Walter Darby Bannard

The most singular fact about the Barbara Johnson Collection was that it consisted not of one type of object, but of hundreds of different types of object all relating to a central subject: whales and whaling. It was less a collection of things than a section of life, a physical chronicle of an activity, in which human and natural history had been pieced back together. Thus one found within this huge assemblage, books, prints, manuscripts, paintings, tools, models, weathervanes, furniture and carvings. Barbara Johnson says she often did not know what she was looking for until she found it.

Scrimshaw is the folk art of the whaleman and was therefore an essential part of the collection. The term embraces objects made of materials taken from whales: whales' teeth; whalebone, from the jaw of the sperm whale, including pan bone, the very dense, thin, flat bone from the joint region; and baleen, the flexible, plastic-like plates taken from the mouths of baleen whales. It may also include wood, walrus ivory and other marine materials.

Great care was taken in selecting scrimshaw for the collection, both to screen out the fakes and the non-scrimshaw bone and ivory, and also to select discriminately from the great quantity of scrimshaw that was coming on to the market at the time Barbara Johnson began collecting. The task was particularly difficult as scrimshaw has no history, almost no known artists because it is seldom signed, and no clear scheme of dating. The literature was mostly guesswork, so the only tangible points of reference were scrimshaw in museums or in the hands of dealers, and one's own ability to learn from mistakes.

The first piece of scrimshaw that Barbara Johnson acquired was an engraved tooth, one of a pair. Her primary interest at the time was printed historical material and, at first, she felt that one tooth was enough. Soon she went back to buy the second, but it had been sold – she has been looking for it ever since. It was then she learned that a collector seldom regrets what she buys, only what she has not bought.

As time went on, the outlines of the subject gained in clarity and detail. It became possible to identify prisoner-of-war and Oriental carving, and the various kinds of bone and ivory, carved and engraved in so many ways for so many centuries, all of which seemed to come with the hopeful label 'scrimshaw'. The collection grew to contain more than 2,000 pieces, including hundreds of outstanding examples of common types; busks, swifts, whaling scenes engraved on teeth, jagging wheels and canes.

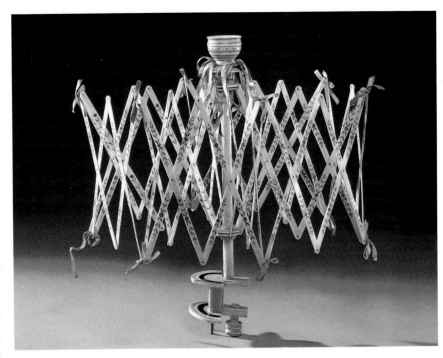

Fig 2
An American engraved polychrome scrimshaw whalebone and whale-ivory
swift, *circa* 1845, height 13in (33cm)
New York $6,600 (£3,687). 12.XII.81
From the collection of Barbara Johnson

Fig 1 *Left*
An American engraved polychrome scrimshaw whalebone busk, inscribed,
circa 1840, length 12½in (31.8cm)
New York $6,600 (£3,687). 12.XII.81
From the collection of Barbara Johnson

Decorative corset stays, or 'busks', were popular courting gifts and a preferred
form for the scrimshander. The busk illustrated here (Fig 1), which came to be called
the 'unity busk', was Barbara Johnson's own favourite. It was made *circa* 1840 from
pan bone, and it is almost an inventory of pictorial scrimshaw themes of the time: the
American eagle and flag, the dove of peace, the square-rigged ship, Calliope with her
lyre, and the angel of mercy. The engraving, done with a sail needle and filled with
coloured pigments, is typical of the best of its kind. Although 'primitive' in design, it
has a muscular calligraphy and sureness that puts most commercial illustration of the
period to shame. There are examples in the literature of engraved scrimshaw by the
same hand, which give rare clues to the identity of the artist, the ship on which he
sailed and the likely date of engraving. A similar busk bears the name *J. V. Booth*, and
the inscription *M Ann* on this piece may refer to the *Mary Ann* which made six
voyages from Fairhaven, Massachusetts, between 1838 and 1858.

Fig 3
An American inlaid mahogany scrimshaw vanity chest, *circa* 1880,
width 14¼in (36.2cm)
New York $9,900 (£5,531). 12.XII.81
From the collection of Barbara Johnson

The swift, a complicated piece of machinery which held a hank of yarn so that it could be wound into a ball, was another common type of scrimshaw and might be said to be the test of an advanced scrimshander. The whalebone, whale-ivory and tortoise-shell swift illustrated here (Fig 2) is exceptional for its fine proportions and grace, and for the engraved slats, which are a very rare feature. Made at about the same time as the busk, it is as much an inventory of scrimshaw-making techniques as the busk is of scrimshaw motifs, incorporating carving, engraving, turning, joining, rivetting and inlay. The pretty grey and yellow ribbons are original. Like the busk, which is engraved with the legend *Remember Me When Far Away*, the swift was probably a gift for someone at home.

In the early nineteenth century, scrimshaw engraving had tended to be graceful and calligraphic, and carving was trim and spare. Later, engraving became denser and more rigid, and carving often became complex to the point of rococo, as exemplified by a magnificent vanity chest (Fig 3), made *circa* 1880. It is fashioned from hundreds of pieces of exotic wood, whale ivory, whalebone, baleen, abalone shell, copper and silver. The complexity does not stop with the sparkling contrasts of the surface inlay,

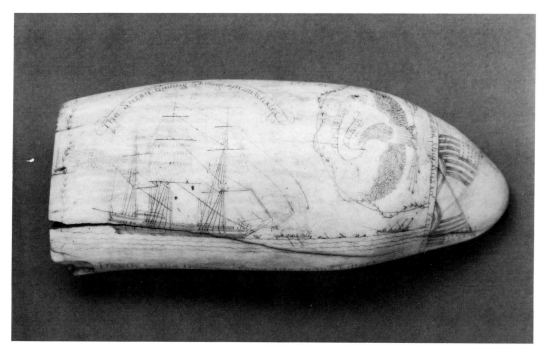

Fig 4
An American scrimshaw whale's tooth engraved by Frederick Myrick, inscribed, signed and dated
Feb. the 9th 1829, length 6in (15.2cm)
New York $11,000 (£6,145). 12.XII.81
From the collection of Barbara Johnson

but extends to the construction. There are four small drawers and a large drawer in the front of the box, and lifting the hinged top reveals six more drawers, a secret compartment and a mirror. It is a *tour de force* of extravagant Victorian craftsmanship.

A search for the special and unique began once the collection had filled up with the favourite forms of the scrimshander. It soon became evident that the more unusual the item, the more the ordinary collector shied away from it. That is why the most expensive scrimshaw are the famous 'Susan's teeth', which are not only typical and celebrated, but also the only scrimshaw known to have been done in series (Fig 4). About eighteen teeth have been found, all engraved, signed, dated and inscribed by Frederick Myrick on board the ship *Susan* of Nantucket, in 1828 and 1829.

A scrimshaw chess set was once scorned by most bidders at a New England auction because, while elephant-ivory chess sets were common, whale-ivory chess sets were known only from whaling journals. It was assumed that it was not 'right'. Barbara Johnson bought this set amid much scoffing for a fraction of its real value. At the same sale, on the other hand, she paid dearly for a set of whalebone door knobs, simply because one other collector had, like herself, looked past the rough carving to recognize how unique and interesting they were as scrimshaw.

The Barbara Johnson Collection was the largest private collection in the world, not only of scrimshaw, but of everything relating to whales, whaling and whalers. It is improbable that its like will ever be dispersed again.

Wine

A silver-plated wine carriage
by Christofle & Cie,
nineteenth century
London £320 ($573). 30.IX.81

The season has again been very active. In addition to the regular London programme of nineteen sales, others took place in Chester, Pulborough, Chicago and Geneva with a net total of £2,301,552 ($4,119,778), an increase of 8.44 percent over the previous season. The eighth annual sale at Nederburg, Cape Province, South Africa, achieved another record total, of R719,000 (£372,539:$666,845).

The first sale of the season was devoted to red and white Burgundies offered by Morgan Furze, agents for the wine merchants, Bouchard Père et Fils. Later in September, a magnificent cellar shipped from an hotel north of Dijon attracted a great deal of attention, along with the directors' reserve of a London merchant, which included an Imperial of Château Mouton Rothschild 1929. The entire cellars of the Bath Club came up for sale in October. The first sale of wine to be held by the company in the United States took place at the Drake Hotel, Chicago, on 17 November. It comprised a collection of fine and rare wines owned by Vintage Imports Inc, and sold for a total of £423,919 ($758,815). In December, another well-known French hotelier's stocks, from the Vosges, were offered and in a sale the following May a special section was devoted to Madeira, in order to promote the greater appreciation of these versatile wines. They may be served before or after a meal and once a bottle has been opened the contents will not deteriorate for several months. Other rare items sold this season include several bottles from the estates of the Princes of Prussia at Schloss Reinhartshausen, West Germany, and a recently discovered nineteenth-century English cellar of wines, spirits, cordials and delft bin labels.

The market has been particularly strong in 1961, 1966 and 1970 first and classed growth Clarets. Also strong have been 1945, 1960 and 1963 vintage Ports and Rhône wines. German wines and Burgundies have been vulnerable to the recession and present the greatest bargains. This trend is likely to continue in the coming season.

From left to right
Château Mouton Rothschild 1929, CB (one Imperial). London £4,400 ($7,876). 30.IX.81
Cognac Napoléon, Grande Fine Champagne 1811, OB (one large bottle, approx half gallon).
London £1,000 ($1,790). 2.VI.82
Extrait d'Absinthe, OB, Pernod Fils, Tarragona, probably before 1939 (one litre).
London £180 ($322). 2.VI.82
Tokay Essence 1888, OB (one half litre). London £160 ($286). 2.VI.82
Constantia, *circa* 1860 (one half bottle), with circular lead bottle marker embossed *Red Constantia*.
London £120 ($215). 2.VI.82

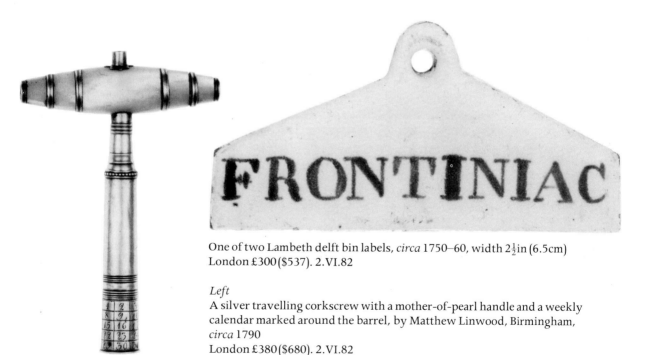

One of two Lambeth delft bin labels, *circa* 1750–60, width $2\frac{1}{2}$in (6.5cm)
London £300 ($537). 2.VI.82

Left
A silver travelling corkscrew with a mother-of-pearl handle and a weekly
calendar marked around the barrel, by Matthew Linwood, Birmingham,
circa 1790
London £380 ($680). 2.VI.82

Notes on contributors

Clive Aslet is senior architectural writer for *Country Life*. He has recently published a book on English country houses from 1890 to 1939, *The Last Country Houses* (1982).

Walter Darby Bannard is an artist and writer. He has had considerable experience collecting and researching scrimshaw and other whaling artifacts. He has written many articles for art journals and is writing a book on scrimshaw, to be published in the near future.

Maurice Byrne is an Honorary Research Fellow in the Department of Physics at Warwick University. He has published a number of papers on the history of woodwind and brass instruments and their makers in the Galpin Society Journal.

Manolis Chatzidakis, formerly Director of both the Byzantine and the Benaki museums, Athens, is the foremost living icon historian of Greece. The author of numerous articles and books, he has specialized in the post-Byzantine period. Among his most important books are a catalogue of the icons in the Hellenic Institute, Venice (1962), *Icons of Patmos* (1977) and his *Etude sur la Peinture post-Byzantine* (reprinted 1976).

William H. Gerdts is Professor of History of Art at Brooklyn College and the Graduate School of the City University of New York. He was Curator of Painting and Sculpture at the Newark Museum, New Jersey and Associate Professor of Art and Gallery Director at the University of Maryland, before assuming his present post. He has produced many exhibition catalogues and articles, and is the author of several books, including *Washington Allston* (1979), *American Impressionism* (1980) and *Painters of the Humble Truth* (1981).

David James is Islamic Curator at the Chester Beatty Library, Dublin. His special interests are Islamic illuminated manuscripts, *Qur'ans* and calligraphy. His most recent publications are *Qur'ans and Bindings from the Chester Beatty Library* (1980) and the catalogue of the Chester Beatty Library Islamic Treasures Exhibition held at Leighton House, London (1981). He is currently writing a book on fourteenth-century Qur'anic calligraphy and illumination in the Near East.

David R. Murray has written extensively on music for the BBC since he joined in 1978. He has contributed articles and reviews to journals and broadcast talks about Wagner on the BBC World Service. His particular interests are Wagner's sketches and *Parsifal*.

Ronald G. Pisano was formerly Director of the Parrish Art Museum, Southampton, New York and is presently an art consultant to private and corporate collectors. He is author of the book *William Merritt Chase* (1979) and is compiling a computerized catalogue raisonné of the artist's work. He has also written articles on Chase and his important students, and organized a number of exhibitions relating to the artist. He has published articles and exhibition catalogues on other important nineteenth and twentieth-century American artists.

Walter Spiegl has written several books on antiques, including two on Biedermeier and nineteenth-century glass. He is an editor with the German art magazine *Weltkunst* for which he also writes articles, mainly on glass and ceramics. At the moment, he is working on a study of glass decorated by Samuel Mohn and Anton Kothgasser in Vienna.

Eunice Williams was formerly acting Curator of Drawings at the Fogg Art Museum, Harvard University. She has researched, organized and catalogued major exhibitions in America, including Gods and Heroes: Baroque Images of Antiquity (1968), and an exhibition of Fragonard drawings in North American collections for the National Gallery of Art, Washington DC (1978–79). She has been researching into Fragonard for many years and is preparing further articles on the artist.

Mark Winter is a collector and dealer in Navajo and related textiles and has often written and lectured on the subject. He is responsible for the organization of the Durango Collection, Durango, Colorado and advises other museums, as well as educational and financial institutions.

Mark Zebrowski is an authority in the field of Indian art. He has published several articles on Indian decorative arts and his book *Deccani Painting* will appear in 1983. He is also preparing books on Indian metalware and Rajasthani painting.

John Hayward is a consultant to Sotheby's and the following contributors are experts with the company: Christopher de Hamel, Robert Kleiner and John Vaughan (in London); Letitia Roberts (in New York).

NICOLAES VAN VEERENDAEL
A tulip, carnations and morning glory in a glass vase
Signed, 17in by 13in (43.2cm by 33cm)
London £55,000 ($98,450). 9.XII.81
From the collection of the late Mrs Barbara Agar

Index

A Mamluk leather shadow puppet of a horse and groom, Egypt, late thirteenth–early fourteenth century, width 27in (68.5cm)
New York $7,150(£3,994). 10.XII.81
From the collection of T. B. Kahle